C0-ART-111

TO DO WITH BIRDS

TO DO WITH BIRDS

By

HENRY TEGNER, M.A.

With Illustrations by
D. WATKINS-PITCHFORD ("B.B.")

HERBERT JENKINS : LONDON

First published by
Herbert Jenkins Ltd.
3 Duke of York Street
London, S.W.1
1965

MADE AND PRINTED IN GREAT BRITAIN BY
JOHN GARDNER (PRINTERS) LTD., HAWTHORNE ROAD, LIVERPOOL, 20.

FOR

WILLIAM MARSHALL

OF

COIRE CAS
NETHYBRIDGE

FOREWORD

I SUPPOSE IT is entirely wrong to start off a book by saying what
it does not purport to be, but it would be unfair to the possible
purchaser of this volume, or its intending borrower at the library, to find that instead of a catalogue of British birds or a
work on bird recognition he finds himself with a book of personal reminiscences, for that, in fact, is what this is. I have been
interested in birds ever since I was given a sparrow's egg by an
older boy when I could hardly tell the difference between an
egg and a glass marble. I am sure that, at the time, I would
have preferred the marble.

I remember, too, the first time I shot a red-legged partridge
in Norfolk with a single-barrelled four-ten gun. Yes, I suppose
I have been in my time one of those much castigated hunter-
naturalists. I can recall, even now, the scarlet of that partridge's beak and legs and its lovely plumage. I saw my last
red-legged partridge in the hills behind C'as Catala in the
Balearic island of Mallorca. I was just as thrilled as I had been
nearly fifty years ago.

When one takes an interest in birds one naturally sees all one
possibly can of them and I have found that I am almost as keen
to read everything I can about them. Fortunately for those of us
who live in the British Isles it is well-supplied with very efficient libraries so that anyone can learn about birds through
reading as well as by watching. The two are really concomitant.

During a life-time of interest in birds I have come across a
number of intriguing problems. For example do certain members of the owl family carry their young as woodcocks do?
I have never seen an owl do this as I have a woodcock carry its
chick but certain writers have suggested that infant-portage is
a habit of the owl family.

Did that great grouse bird, the capercaille, actually become
extinct in this country as most ornithologists accept or did he
linger on in token numbers in some primeval Scottish forest?

Is the golden eagle the figure of majesty he is always made out to be or is he more of a carrion eater like the raven and the crow?

Today more people take an interest in birds than ever before and there are certain factors which have helped to intensify this situation. The Press, the B.B.C. and the "Telly" have all found that birds can be popular subjects and they have consequently boosted them. Men like James Fisher, David Attenborough and Peter Scott have helped the public to become bird-conscious.

To many of us who are fortunate enough to live in the country birds are a source of constant pleasure but the townsman, too, can watch birds either by getting into the country during week-ends—and with modern methods of quick transport there are few of us who cannot do so. But even in the suburbs, the towns and the cities there are millions of birds today. The list of British birds is so vast that to write at any length about them all would fill a library. These few notes therefore deal with a limited number. Anyone can choose the bird he likes and even with only one species he can easily make a life-time study of his choice—many men, in fact, have done just this.

CONTENTS

CONTENTS

ACKNOWLEDGMENTS

Some of the material contained in this book has appeared in *The Times*, *The Field*, *Countryman*, *Birds Illustrated*, *Birds & Country*, *Scotland's Magazine*, and the *C.G.A. Magazine*. To the editors of all these publications I am duly grateful for their permission to reprint.

H.T.

TO DO WITH BIRDS

* 1 *

THE CHIEFTAIN GROUSE

IN A CLEARING in the ancient forest of Abernethy the giant
grouse strutted and clicked. Against the russet background of a
bracken-clad mound he looked almost as big as a turkey-cock
in his shining garb of purple and turquoise green. His great
wings trailed, rustling the dead stalks of the bracken, whilst he
called *pick-up*, *pick-up*, *pick-up* with increasing rapidity to end
quickly his love-serenade with a sudden *plop*, as if a cork had
been neatly withdrawn from a bottle of champagne. During
his display the cock capercaille drooped his eyelids in his ecstasy
so that only the shining slits of his jet-black pupils showed
between the eyes' membranes. Somewhere in the bracken a hen
crouched, she was not yet prepared to submit herself to the
chieftain's chanting. The courtship dance of the capercaille is
referred to as his *play* whereas in the case of his near cousin the
blackcock, this is usually termed the *lek*. The name capercaille
is of Gaelic origin, being derived from the words *cabhar-coille* or
bird of the woods just as *cabhar-athar* means, in the same language, a snipe or bird of the ether. It was the ancient Scots who
gave the caper, because of his size, the rank of chieftain grouse.

That the capercaille was once a bird native to these islands
there is no doubt and there is in existence in the Hancock
Natural History Museum, in Newcastle upon Tyne, a stuffed
specimen of a cock capercaille which is said to be an indigenous
bird. This specimen is believed to have been acquired by one
of the Hancock brothers from the Tunstall private natural
history museum in Yorkshire. However, there is a certain
amount of doubt as to the authenticity of this relic and it has
been suggested that the original owner of the Tunstall museum
may have obtained this specimen from a dealer, believing, in
all good faith, that the capercaille he had acquired was a

genuine Scotsman; whereas, in fact, the bird had come from Scandinavia, where caper are plentiful and never became extinct as they unfortunately did in this country, at the end of the eighteenth, or the beginning of the nineteenth century. There appears to be some doubt as to the exact date of this extinction for some authorities give this as about 1769 whilst others maintain that capercailles survived in western Inverness-shire and in the Glenmoriston woodlands until 1815. If the latter date can be taken as approximately correct then there was a very short period of time before capers were re-introduced into Scotland—less than 25 years, in fact—because in 1837 Lord Breadalbane, after consultations with Sir Thomas Fowill Buxton, purchased a number of adult capercailles in Sweden and had them brought over to Scotland. This purchase was arranged through a Mr. Lloyd, who was a resident in Sweden. Laurence Banville, a gamekeeper, was chosen to go over the North Sea to collect the birds. Fifty four adult capercailles, of different sexes, were successfully shipped to Scotland, in a schooner, in the expert care of Laurence Banville and were eventually released—presumably in much the same way that artificially bred pheasants are released today—in the wooded districts of the Tay valley.

The brevity of this period of extinction, i.e. 22 years has, I admit, often tempted me to wonder, as I have walked in the primeval pine forests of Rothiermurchus and Abernethy, whether, in fact, a few odd caper did not manage to survive in Scotland and that some of the many birds one sees these days, in these districts, are descendants of our original stock, but then I am an incorrigible sentimentalist.

The introduction into Scotland of birds from the Scandinavian countries, however, did prove an undoubted success because, subsequent to the Breadalbane-Buxton experiment, others followed so that there were a number of caper introductions during the latter half of the nineteenth century into various places in Scotland.

Subsequently, attempts were made to bring the caper back to parts of England where originally he was also a native. The bones of capercailles have been found in the northern English counties and elsewhere. Lord Ravensworth, who was, inciden-

tally, a great introducer—he tried to bring into Northumberland such species as the beaver and the reindeer—obtained some caper eggs from Scotland. These were successfully hatched off on his own estate at Eslington where the birds were eventually released. Remnants of this experiment survived for several years but they were finally exterminated; it is suggested by some naturalists that shooting was responsible but there is no definite proof of this. Sir H. Graham also tried to establish the caper in Cumberland with what success, I do not know. There were, undoubtedly, other attempts as well of this sort, in different parts of the country many of which have never been recorded. Today, there are none of these magnificent grouse birds south of the English-Scottish border and yet it is a state of affairs which should not be difficult to correct if anyone had a mind to do so.

I have often wondered why the Ravensworth introduction of Scottish caper into Northumberland did not succeed. I now believe it was largely because there was neither a sufficiency of conifer woods, of a large enough area, to hold the birds. The situation, today, is entirely different for in Northumberland, and in the adjacent counties of Dumfriess-shire, Cumberland and Durham, there are vast extents of pine woods. I can see no reason why caper should not do well in all these counties and in many others in Britain and Wales, as well, from as far north as Northumberland to the south-western county of Devon. The Forestry Commission, and also many private landowners, have planted great parts of Britain with trees since 1919, here to hand, therefore, is the natural habitat of the capercaille.

A study has been made of the caper's diet. It is very varied, worms, insects, ant's eggs, berries of all sorts, oak-leaves, acorns, birch-buds, heather tops, oats and shoots of Scots fir being represented. It is the last-named item of the caper's diet which has largely prevented any attempts to re-introduce this bird to domains where he is unknown today, for the forester naturally does not want his plantations devastated by flocks of huge turkey-like birds.

However, there are very definite indications, nowadays, that the Forestry Commission, who is, by far, the largest single planter in the United Kingdom, is quite prepared to allow certain animals and birds, who are only partially destructive to their woodlands, to live and survive.

It would indeed be a most interesting and perhaps even rewarding experiment if a number of capercailles could be introduced to suitable woodlands in say Surrey, Devon, Cumberland, Durham, Northumberland and Norfolk so as to see how they acclimatised themselves. The birds would have to be protected for a period of from three to five years, when they might well become a definite sporting asset. After all, artificially planted pine-woods are not over-prolific in the game they are able to provide and, further, such an experiment would not necessarily cost very much.

Game-breeding and game-rearing have taken enormous strides during the present century. If men in the early eighties could successfully introduce caper from over the North Sea into Scotland then I am sure our present-day experts could equally easily scatter a most fascinating and exciting game bird still further afield in this country, even if the caper is not a particularly appetising morsel on the dining-room table. But how exciting it would be to see a huge cock capercaille come gliding over the Bagshot road during a week-end traffic jam.

★ 2 ★

BLACKGROUSE

VERY EARLY one April morning, when motoring along A.697 over Longramlington Moor on my way to Edinburgh from Newcastle upon Tyne, I began to hear an unusual humming sound which, at first, I associated with some part of the mechanism of my car. It had a peculiar rhythm about it rather as if one of the wheels was out of alignment and was rubbing against a part of the chassis. Switching off the engine I brought the car to a stop. The sound went on. A penetrating ululation, with the suggestion of a curlew's call in it, kept sounding.

Looking out of the car, over the moor, I saw, on a bright-green knoll, four hundred yards across the heather, two bouncing balls of white, which I recognised at once as the rear-ends of blackcocks on the rut. The rhythmic sound which had first attracted my attention was the spring-song of these birds. The variety of descriptions given to the love-song of the blackcock is quite remarkable. Some writers have claimed that it resembles the long-drawn cooing of the ring dove without the high notes. One author in writing about these birds has suggested that their prolonged mating calls are like a number of tom cats miaowing in the distance. J. G. Millais, the famous bird artist and writer, in his book *Game Birds and Shooting Sketches*, a quarter of which is devoted to the blackgrouse, suggests that the song is rather like the noise of a loaded goods-train running over loose rails at a great distance. This description is far from ludicrous as the continuous cadence of the song has something in common with the rhythmic murmur of wheels passing over lengths of rail. All who have the blackcocks' calling agree that it has a considerable carrying capacity. On a still morning it may be heard for miles around. Sometimes the song is interrupted and before the assembled birds take up the tune again the singers will emit two or three harsh croaks rather like those of a raven. These sudden ejaculations are often made when a new arrival puts in an appearance at the *lekking* ground. Whether they are a form of greeting or a challenge is a matter for conjecture. During the *lek*, or mating display, the cocks bounce, strut and fight. The white rump feathers, which resemble great, swans'-down powder-puffs, are flaunted and the lyre-shaped tail feathers become erect. On a clear morning these white discs can be seen a long way against the sombre background of moorland. They are, in fact, the most usual advertisement of the blackcocks' mating places. To watch these birds perform always puts me in mind of some fantastic tribal mating dance of black savages, if there are any such still left in this world. The glistening blue-black plumage of the magnificent cocks and their strutting, stomping and circling, accompanied by the persistant ululation of their music, which has something of the tom-tom in it, all seem to combine to give the impression of some primitive performance.

Sometimes a cock will sing on his own. One day, also on Longframlington Moor, I saw a cock perched on the wooden fence beside the road. He was in full throat bubbling away with much vigour. His neck was outstretched and his scarlet wattles aflame as he chortled away at his love-song. He appeared quite oblivious of my presence. I looked for a greyhen but saw no sign of her.

Subsequently I discovered two more *lekking* sites in this area. There is no doubt that these stomping grounds are regularly resorted to and presumably always by the same birds. It is really remarkable how seldom one sees the hens about in the neighbourhood of these displaying places. Admittedly the greyhen is a very dowdy bird, when compared with her gorgeous mate, and the drab plumage of the female makes her more difficult to spot but even with her camouflage it should be possible to pick her out if she were somewhere about.

That hens attend the early spring *leks* there is no doubt but as the cocks seem to go on with their tribal performances well into the summer months the hens by then will be presumably occupied with their domestic affairs. The greyhen, after she has been initially covered, will lay, brood, and then hatch out her eggs and the subsequent care of her young will occupy her well into the summer.

The greyhen has wrongly been accused of being a negligent mother. This is another case of "giving a dog a bad name" for the greyhen is no more neglectful a mother than is the hen red grouse or the hen pheasant. The greyhen may even possibly be a better parent than the latter. The greyhen, however, lives in terrain particularly favoured by vermin, for the edges of moors and marginal lands are the rearing places of many predators. Further, long, rank heather and deep, sheer-sided, draining ditches, cut by monstrous mechanical diggers, are hazards which few mothers can cope with whilst their young ones are still unfledged.

Blackcocks have been called "beany" birds and if their *lekking* performances are a true indication of their sexual abilities then they certainly deserve the appellation for male black-grouse will go on with their so-called mating displays well into the autumnal months. Some naturalists regard these fall performances as a form of erotomania. I have seen several of these late year gatherings and one in particular which took place regularly at Upper Tullochghru in the forest of Rothiemurchus in Inverness-shire. Here a dozen or more cocks would strut and feather as if the month was April and not late October.

Mr. Harold Evetts, who used to live at Porlock in Somerset, happened to write me an account of blackcocks *lekking* on Exmoor a few days after I had witnessed a similar event in Inverness-shire. Evetts described the song of these autumn displaying birds as *bubbly-jay, bubbly-jock* continued *ad infinitum*. This particular *lek* went on for at least an hour after sunrise.

I think that here in Northumberland and, perhaps, in some of the Border counties there has been a slow but steady increase in the numbers of these birds over the past decade. This, if it is a fact, is a good thing for in the past Northumberland was known to some ornithologists as the "Cradle of the Blackcock" but its reputation as such has surely suffered in subsequent years as these birds have dwindled in their numbers.

Naturally, one's own observations must, of necessity, be

confined to a limited area and the fact that one individual notices, what appears to be a gradual increase in his district, does not necessarily mean that this is general. However, the combined findings of a number of observers has encouraged me to hope that blackgrouse are now on the advance. As forests are planted, on virgin terrain and grow up, the territory becomes unsuitable for these birds and consequently with the general increase in afforestation it is likely that the numbers of blackgrouse will rather dwindle than otherwise but we who love these splendid, boisterous grouse birds can only hope that they will continue to survive to grace this wild northern county of ours.

At certain times of year blackgame, like the red grouse, are inclined to pack. They will also combine to make short migratory flights. These mass movements make it difficult to assess numbers correctly. Blackgrouse, on occasion, turn up in the most surprising places.

J. G. Millais, in one of his books, states that British blackgrouse do not migrate like the Continental birds. The latter evidently will travel considerable distances during the late autumn and winter months. These voyages on the part of massed blackgame are, Millais believes, entirely a movement in search of food. Almost exactly the same sort of thing happens in Northumberland only on a much smaller scale. Here in October and November the blackgrouse commence to gather. There appears to be no sex segregation about these collections. On one occasion I saw a mass flight of both sexes, numbering over seventy birds, flying at an estimated altitude of between 300 and 400 feet, over the Cheviot foothills in a south-easterly direction. The birds appeared to be heading for the Coquet valley.

On another occasion I watched a pack of twenty-two greyhen on Cragside Moor, above the town of Rothbury, the weather was mild and clear, the month January. On seeing me the birds rose in a mass from the heather where they had been feeding on something. Keeping close together they now circled, gradually climbing all the time, until they were over the tall conifers around Cragside house when they set course again in a south-easterly direction.

These birds appear to have regular flight routes probably between daytime feeding grounds and their evening roosting spots. Every winter, between the beginning of December and the middle of January blackgrouse fly from off the moors above the Coquet valley, where presumably they breed and live during the summer, to the lowlands about Longhorsley Moor some six miles to the north of Morpeth on the A.1 road. The attraction which causes this local migration is undoubtedly the heavy berry crops usually to be found on the unkempt hedges around Longhorsley Moor.

Until recently the professional forester was death on blackgame because this bird was considered to be particularly destructive to newly-planted conifer seedlings. Birds found on forestry land were destroyed out of hand. Nests when found were heeled in. If any birds got away with a brood they were hammered pretty hard with the shotgun. It is surprising that so many birds have survived. Now, I am glad to say, the attitude of the forester towards these birds appears to be undergoing a change. Foresters, like all of us, appreciate seeing wild life about for a forest denuded of all living things can be a dreary, depressing place. There is no finer ornament to a glade in the woods than the sight of a glorious, shining blackgrouse with his eyelids aflame and his tail erect strutting, like some woodland hobgoblin, to the tune of his full-throated bubbling song.

★ 3 ★

PTARMIGAN

I saw my first ptarmigan, in what is now the National Forest Park of Glenmore, long before Glenmore became established in 1948 as a National Forest Park.

I was on the slopes of Mam Suim with Murdo McKenzie, the stalker from Glenmore Lodge. It was a day of mist and the wisps of damp moisture periodically blotted out the scenery around us. We had stopped to allow the mist to clear a little before proceeding towards the summit of Mam Suim. Suddenly out of the fog came a peculiar sound which echoed in the high corries—*wee-ac, wee-ac*—it came again and then, in a momentary clearing of the vapour, I saw three white, bat-like forms go slithering out of our sight over a tumble of huge, granite boulders. The croaking sound of these birds' voices was just as if someone had rubbed two pieces of stone together.

"Peter-miggen", Murdo McKenzie whispered.

"Peter-miggen—snow grouse", he added.

It took me a minute or two before I grasped what he was saying. Murdo always referred to pneumonia as "peenie-moanie" so that I realised "peter-miggen" was his way of pronouncing ptarmigan.

That first sight of ptarmigan gave me an interest in them which has never diminished during the many years I have been lucky enough to be able to watch and study them.

Comparatively few people have ever seen a ptarmigan and this is not at all surprising when it is realised that these grouse of the high mountain ranges seldom descend below the 1500 foot level.

The ptarmigan, *Lagopus mutus*, has the most distinct colour-change of any of our native grouse. During the winter months most of these birds assume a snow-white plumage whilst in the

25

summer the wings mainly remain white when the body feathers assume a grey or yellow tinge not unlike the colour of the granite scree amongst which these creatures spend most of their time. Rather surprisingly there is still argument as to whether ptarmigan have white wing feathers all through the year. *The Field Guide to the Birds of Britain & Europe*, published by Collins, says, without equivocation, that at *all* seasons they may be distinguished by white wings and white belly—the emphasising of the word *all* is mine. The great bird illustrator, G. E. Lodge, however, in his lovely picture of ptarmigan in summer plumage, which illustrates *British Sporting Birds* by F. B. Kirkman and Horace G. Hutchinson, shows these birds without white wings or bellies. My own observation of ptarmigan during the summer months has been that they always have white wings. Above the eye itself there is a membrane of vivid blood-red which becomes even more brilliant, in the cock-bird, during the breeding period. I have never seen a ptarmigan in captivity although I have read somewhere that ptarmigan are easy birds to rear; however, I do not believe this.

Ptarmigan have the biggest wings, when compared with the body, of any of our game birds, this makes them strong fliers but they are also expert runners capable of scuttling over the barren tundra of the high places at high speed. Young ptarmigan are precocious birds who are able to fly very early in their careers and when they reach the size of a thrush they appear to be able to keep up quite well, in flight, with their parents.

One year, during the 1939–45 war, when I was on leave in Glen Einich I spent a day in Corrie Ruadh and Corrie Beinnhe, two of the best ptarmigan corries in the Grampian range, the birds that year were late and in September there were many tiny mites about. It was astonishing to see how strongly these fledgling grouse could fly.

The ptarmigan appear to change their diet with the seasons for in the summer insects form a large part of their intake whilst in the autumn the many varieties of berries are resorted to with relish. Later, in the winter, the leaves of dwarf plants, and whatever else that can be found beneath the snow and amongst the frozen scree, are eaten by these amazingly hardy birds. Ptarmigan can live under snow for considerable periods and, like the Eskimo, in his ice igloo, they appear to keep warm enough to survive beneath their covering of snow. Like their bigger cousins, the red and blackgrouse, ptarmigan have the habit of packing through the late autumn. These packs are made up of a number of families, or coveys as the sportsman calls them, which have herded together. Such concentrations would seem to come about as a result of the availability of certain feeding stuffs in a particular locality.

Although there is no direct evidence to prove it, the ptarmigan seem to have been more numerous, a hundred years ago, in Scotland than they are today. I say no direct evidence as no attempts have ever been made to ascertain the past or present ptarmigan-population of this country. However, when one reads the sporting books of the 19th century one cannot help but come to the conclusion that ptarmigan were not only plentiful in certain localities but also that they were fairly widespread. In the Western Islands and the west-coastal, mountainous regions of Scotland these mountain grouse would seem, once, to have been quite numerous whereas, now, this is not the case. Why this should be so it is a little difficult to understand because most certainly ptarmigan shooting is less popular today than it was in the day of Hawker, St. John, Speedy and Colquhoun.

It may possibly be that the ptarmigan's natural enemies, excluding man, have increased. The eagle and the peregrine are not by any means uncommon north of the Border. There are certainly more carrion crows and ravens since the keeper-population of the Highlands has diminished. Eagles and peregrines kill adult birds, whereas ravens and carrion crows enjoy the eggs and chicks of the ptarmigan. Then there is that present-day menace of the hills the black-backed gull who has learnt that there is a plethora of carrion and other good feeding inland rather than out at sea. Weather and nature's predators take a far greater toll of the numbers of ptarmigan than any number of shooters.

In March 1950 I had to go to Sweden on business. I decided to take a small cargo boat from Hull to Gothenburg. This vessel had on board a cargo of tractors destined for Stavanger in Norway. We struck one of the worst storms I have ever experienced which delayed us for twenty-four hours. On arrival at Stavanger the tractors had to be unloaded and whilst this was going on I went up to the natural history museum, which is situated above the town of Stavanger, as at that time I was doing some research on the hybridisation of grouse. I was taken by one of the attendants in the museum to meet the curator Dr. Holger Holgersen who was the only man in the place who could speak English and he speaks it beautifully. On Dr. Holgersen's desk was the tow-stuffed skin of a ptarmigan in full winter plumage. I think it was that bird that sealed our friendship for I have kept in touch with Dr. Holgersen ever since my first meeting with him and we have exchanged a good many letters on subjects of mutual interest from seals to kelp-pigeons. On the subject of ptarmigan Dr. Holgersen is in a class by himself. I had no idea how valuable this bird was in the economy of Norway. It is regarded extremely highly as a game bird by the sporting community and there are more shooters today than there have ever been before. In November when the birds become very wild and the shooting season is virtually over snaring commences. The snaring of ptarmigan with brass-wire or horse-hair nooses is a skilled occupation but it is merely a method used to take these birds for marketing purposes. During the last century enormous numbers of ptarmigan were exported from Norway to Britain.

In March 1840 a single game dealer in Leadenhall market is said to have received 15,000 birds from Norway and 60,000 birds in a single season from Lapland. A Norwegian dealer may well dispose of over 50,000 ptarmigan in a year, most of which now go to Denmark, Sweden and Germany. Very few if any of these mountain grouse come to Britain now, although there may be occasional consignments into Leith or Aberdeen where small quantities of ptarmigan are still sold by the game dealers.

In the Scandinavian countries and on the Continent of Europe the ptarmigan is very highly regarded as a table delicacy. As the retail price of the bird is high, at the present time, there is a much better market for the Norwegians and the Laplanders abroad than there is here where the ptarmigan, as a table bird, takes a very back-seat when compared with the red grouse. That the ptarmigan was greatly appreciated by our forefathers, however, there is no doubt because in *The Lady of the Lake* by Sir Walter Scott, there is this couplet:

> "O'er Ptarmigan and Venison
> The Priest had spoke his benison"

Ptarmigan, like all the grouse family, appear to be subject to considerable annual fluctuations in numbers. Professor Holgersen believes that there is a more marked fluctuation in the seasonal numbers of ptarmigan than of any other game bird. These cycles, he says, vary within a period of 3-4 years and now and then there is a definite peak year which will produce an abnormally large number of these birds.

An inquiry is now underway in this country concerning the red grouse population; this inquiry does not cover the ptarmigan and it is unlikely to do so. The truth is that we do not know much more about this fascinating bird of the high-tops than was known a hundred years ago. This to me, at least, is a very comforting thought.

★ 4 ★

PARTRIDGES

THERE IS NO doubt that amongst the partridges' greatest admirers are the men who shoot them. This love of the creatures man destroys is a curious thing and to suggest that this affection is purely selfish is far from correct. Men like Brian Vesey-Fitzgerald and the late Eric Parker have written with deep feeling about this attractive game bird and they were both shooting men with a great practical knowledge of wild life and a very real affection for the birds and beasts of our countryside. Unfortunately, too many people these days are apt to vilify the sportsman. There is a wide difference between the shooting man, who is generally a protectionist, and the marauding type of gunmen I describe later in this book. It is doubtful whether we would have, in this country, an eighth of the game birds we now have if the shooter, by some circumstance, were to be eliminated.

In the past it has also been the practice for many ardent ornithologists to blame the gamekeeper for the wholesale destruction of birds which are considered harmful to the keeper's mercenary interests. Many gamekeepers today are fairly intelligent people with a far greater knowledge of the ways of the wild than most of us amateur bird watchers. The majority of gamekeepers now do not kill out of hand and a lot of them are just as interested in the behaviour of a kestrel or a partridge as you or I.

This chapter was supposed to deal with the last-named bird but it has gone off the track. However, it is not easy to write of *Perdix perdix* without mentioning his two most enthusiastic adherents, the keeper and the shooting man.

Partridges are mainly monogamous and in the past it was

believed that they paired for life; this may be so, provided that one of the partners is not destroyed, by chemicals, gun, or on the nest by silage cutters, but a bird deprived of its partner will pair again, I am quite sure. The pairing for life theory, I believe, is largely a sentimentalist's story. Once paired, early in the year, these birds appear to be as affectionate as many other avian species but not necessarily more so. Some cock birds assist in incubation; the cock partridge leaves this matter entirely to his mate. The annual cycle of the partridge goes something like this. Towards the end of December the coveys, or family parties, break up. This dispersement may be delayed over several weeks, according to the weather, and even when the birds have paired off they will frequently come together again as a covey, or even coveys, should a severe cold spell intervene before the pre-nidification period commences. These communal gatherings, early in the year, are nearly always brought about by a packing in search of food.

Cock partridges, like a lot of other male birds, stake out their territories prior to the hen's nesting. The area of these territories varies vastly according to the district's total partridge population. A figure of a pair to ten acres has been given as an average density in well populated partridge country. The hen bird usually lays in May and the eggs are hatched off in June but there is, of course, some variation in this matter. Incubation usually lasts some 24 days and as has already been mentioned is entirely the responsibility of the hen. The young are precocious and are able to run almost as soon as they emerge from the egg. The old pair, with their young, stay together as a covey until the break-up after the year's end. Sometimes two coveys will amalgamate. A pair bereft of their nests, or hatched young, may remain together as a separate entity all through the year and this they usually seem to do. These barren pairs may well have been the reason for the "pair-for-life" credo.

Patridges, at certain times of the year, are quite vocal and they seem to talk with one another in almost human tones, *Kup, kup, kup, kup* and then an occasional *zut, zut*. The voice of these birds when speaking, over distances, one covey to another, *Kirrie, kirrie, kirrie, kirrie* or *kar-whit, kar-whit* all make up into quite a vocabulary.

Over a period of years I have tried to make a study of partridges which today largely inhabit hill country and marginal
land where there is, in fact, little actual cultivation. These hill
birds, I have found, are hardy, virile and frequently most
productive birds. I am rather inclined to think that hill partridges tend to have a somewhat darker plumage than the low-
landers who inhabit farmland, I also believe that, on the whole,
the high-landers are lighter, by an ounce or so, than their lowland brethren.

For many years now I have lived in the country where there
are both these kinds of partridges. My own lowland shoot used
to have quite a few partridges on it and on one farm we used to
get anything up to seventeen brace a day; that was admittedly
before this particular farm became modernised. Modernisation
consisted of removing hundreds of yards of natural fences and
substituting wire fences instead, fertilisers were poured on to
the land and after that pesticides. The potato-haulm was
regularly treated every year by chemical sprays, subsequent to
such treatment no living creature was ever flushed from the
stinking spuds. Silage became very much a crop to be cut early
in the nesting season. How any partridges, at all, were able to
survive on this particular modernised farm it is difficult to
understand but a few have done so. The last count I made
showed two small covies of five birds and one of six on 400 acres.
Prior to modernisation the count would run to treble this number if not more.

In contrast, on the hill areas where I shoot there is little
arable land, no silage, and hardly any chemicals. The hill
partridges seem to hold their own during wet springs as well as
dry. This does not imply that my own experience indicates that
marginal land is better for the partridge than cultivated soil,
such as is found generally in Norfolk and Suffolk, but I do
suggest that there is now sufficient evidence that partridges can,
and do, do well on yellow grassland and the fringe of the heather
belt.

Where marginal land exists, alongside cultivated ground, it
is possible that partridges now prefer higher ground to low.
Modern agricultural methods may have driven partridges to
seek new pastures. The birds harried by poisonous sprays,

artificial manures, and mechanical silage cutters may well prefer safer regions where they have established a hill variety of *Perdix perdix*. I am not going to call them *P.p.montana*, or anything like that, but I will say that the partridges of the uplands, where there is little tillage, have adapted themselves remarkably well to their new terrain and in doing so some of these birds have had to change their diet and even nesting habits for there are few hedgerows in the hills. In their process of adaptation to their new territories they may also have altered their plumage slightly as well as their average body weights. Hill birds, after a number of seasons, appear darker than their lowland brethren rather grouse-like, in fact. That these birds have become tougher specimens, in the course of this transition, is possible. Man himself in the process of colonisation has produced some pretty virile nations. *Perdix perdix* may have done the same.

★ 5 ★

THE KING OF BIRDS

THE MIST COMING down from the high-tops magnified the stags so that they looked like enormous pachyderms as they threaded their way, in single file, over the dark peat-hags. Murdo, the head stalker and I lay on our backs in the long heather watching the deer through our glasses hoping they would eventually cross the march into our own forest.

It was the voice of the eagle which first made his presence known to us. A quick, short, yelping sound quite unlike the guttural bark of a questing raven. Suddenly, he appeared above us not a hundred yards away. He hovered in the mist-laden air whilst he twisted his head from side to side as if he were search-ing for something along the bare mountain side. The air current eddying upwards kept him air-borne so that there was scarcely any movement of his great, spatulated wings. When he came nearer to us it was possible to see the rich yellow of the bird's cere setting off the massive curved, black bill and the hazel-brown colour of his penetrating eyes as he turned his head this way and that way. I do not think the bird ever saw us there lying in the heather. He may have mistaken us for a couple of boulders. I was surprised for I knew that the pink of a human face could be seen on a dark moor at a great distance and both Murdo and I had kept our eyes on the bird the whole time he was within our view. At one point the eagle could not have been much more than twenty feet in the air above our heads.

Since my first close-up view of a golden eagle I have watched them on many occasions. I have had eagles quite near to me in the hills of Angus, in Perthshire and in the county of Inverness-shire. One day whilst sitting on the side of the hill above Jock's Road in the Glen of Clova an eagle swooped to within a few feet of where I sat searching the corries opposite for deer. I think this eagle may mave mistaken the colour of my face for some form of offal and he may well have been making a reconnaissance of an easy meal.

Golden eagles are greater scavengers than many people realise and this is perhaps quite natural as no bird has been more publicised in the romantic sense. The golden eagle has earned for himself the title of the King of Birds presumably because of his size and his great wing-span and the undoubted majesty of his flight.

The Reverend F. O. Morris in his *History of British Birds* says that the golden eagle is rather a vulture than a true falcon.

In this country the golden eagles' diet is said to consist largely of mountain hares, ptarmigans, grouse and, in pre-myxomatosis days, rabbits. Seton Gordon, the well-known Scottish naturalist, has once suggested that the extinction of the rabbit might well forestall a lean time for the population of British golden eagles, as it happens myxomatosis, although it struck the rabbit population of the Highlands, has by no means reduced, through starvation, the existing numbers of *Aquila chrysaetos*.

Carrion is not difficult to come by in the Scottish Highlands, in the spring there are dead lambs to be had for the finding. In the spring and summer there are always numbers of dead grouse which have succumbed to the weather, disease or the gun. In the autumn the deerstalker provides the eagle with a glut of grallochs. During the latter part of the winter there are even more grallochs available, as it is the time of the hind-stalking and in most forests more hinds are killed than stags. In competing for the carrion of the hills there is no doubt that the golden eagle is the master scavenger for until he is satisfied he will see off any raven or crow. On a gralloch, a golden eagle can be an almost ludicrous sight, for he will stride rather like a strutting starling all around the tasty morsel in between his guzzling.

Compared with some of the other members of the *falconidae* such as the peregrines, sparrow hawks and merlins the golden eagle is a clumsy hunter. He strikes his prey with his feet with terrific power but he often misses. On a wounded bird, a couched hare, a sitting ptarmigan or a sickly beast he may be quite adequate but with a fast flying desperate prey the eagle is not likely to be so successful.

On one occasion near Loch Ericht I watched a golden eagle attack a skein of grey geese. The geese, in perfect V formation were flying at an altitude of about 3000 feet south-westwards down the middle of the loch. Suddenly a golden eagle appeared, a mere dot in the sky, above the skein. The eagle made a fruitless attack on the leading goose who appeared to dodge his attack quite easily although the eagle's dive disrupted temporarily the perfection of the geese's flight-formation. Whilst the birds were within my sight the golden eagle made two more attacks without any apparent success, the skein of geese merely dipped and dithered and then gathered again to go on their way down the loch.

I have often watched a pair of eagles quartering a grouse moor or hunting along the face of a mountain for ptarmigan and blue hares. I have never seen an eagle successfully pounce a healthy grouse although these birds undoubtedly do take hen grouse when they are nesting or when they are couched and not properly concealed amongst the heather.

Golden eagles have been taught to hawk but they must be unsatisfactory in this respect. I was an elderly officer in the R.A.F., during the 1939–45 war, when the late Captain Knight brought his famous tame golden eagle, Mr. Ramshaw, to our Mess, but whether Mr. Ramshaw was a successful killer I never learnt. I shall always remember the words of a youthful Pilot Officer, who was then engaged in bombing raids over Germany. In the jargon of the flying fraternity he said of Mr. Ramshaw—

"B——dy wizard bird, old boy, a great pranger I'll bet", but whether he was or not was never disclosed. To prang means to destroy, or break, so that this young man was merely commenting upon the eagle's potential destructive capacity.

Golden eagles can play havoc with a grouse-drive and when such is in progress nothing on earth will stop the grouse from

going the wrong way—that is not over the butts—should there
be a pair of eagles above the driven birds. It is no wonder that
eagles are unpopular on grouse moors. That golden eagles are
on the increase in the Highlands of Scotland I do not doubt;
some keepers on Scottish grouse moors even go so far as to say
that there are too many eagles as it is for the continued safety
of their stocks of game. I also have every reason to believe that
an odd eagle or two may well still be taken in traps, although
they are protected birds, but the fox-trap is still a legal instrument in Scotland for the taking of *Vulpes vulpes crucigera* and a
fox-trap is as effective a device for the capture of an eagle as it
is for a fox provided always that it is properly set in a likely
place.

Golden eagles occasionally get their names into the press for
some sensational act or other. Nearly every year the Scottish
papers are able to record an attack on a roedeer or a red deer
by an eagle. I do not doubt that such occurrences happen
now and then but I think that in the majority of these cases the
deer concerned are usually sickly beasts or animals incapacitated by deep snow or avalanches. An odd red deer calf or so
may be taken by a golden eagle, possibly in mistake for a
couchant hare, but should the parent hind come on any such
depredation then I would put my money on the hind every
time. An enraged matron deer can be a very potent enemy
especially when she gets up on her hind legs to use her forefeet
as a pair of flails.

Golden eagles like all others killers must, on occasion, make
mistakes. There is for instance an interesting account of a golden
eagle attacking a wild-cat—the consequent battle must have
been terrific. At any rate the observer was satisfied that both
the cat and the eagle eventually succumbed as a result of their
combat.

There are a number of records of golden eagles taking
unusual prey. The remains of pigs have been found in eagles'
eyries and the Reverend F. O. Morris quotes three instances
of human babies having been carried off. These three cases are
said to have occurred in Orkney, the Shetlands and the Faroes
where the golden eagle, except as an occasional visitant, is now
extinct. Kidnapping by predatory birds has frequently been

reported from such countries as India but these malefactors have not been golden eagles.

Young eagles take a long time to mature and a bird often does not assume full adult plumage until the age of four. They are also believed to be long-lived. The golden eagle of Scotland does not appear to migrate to any extent although Continental birds undoubtedly do so. The now popular practice of bird-ringing has not been used to any extent on our native birds for the difficulties have presumably been too great. Ringing is a useful guide to both migratory habits and longevity but with birds like golden eagles ringing is no easy problem. A pair of golden eagles nested successfully in 1954 in the County of Antrim in Ireland. These birds were almost certainly Scottish emigrants. More recently still a pair is said to have nested in the Lake District, this is encouraging as it might indicate a possible extension of the eagle's territory in the British Isles; at the same time we are a small, overpopulated country and there is not a great deal of available eagle-terrain. Stray eagles occasionally come southwards over the English-Scottish border, a fairly recent visitor was a hen bird who came to Northumberland and stayed in the Christianbury Crags area on the Cumbrian-Northumbrian march for three weeks. This was in 1950. During the period of the eagle's sojourn in England he was under the the constant observation of Harry Earsman of Whickhope, a Scotsman who has spent a good part of his early youth at Ardtornish in Argyllshire so that Earsman knows an eagle when he sees one.

Golden eagles are stated to be multi-nesters. Observers of the nidification of these birds have noticed that eagles have two or even three alternate eyries, as the carrion left eventually makes the nests nauseous places; and it takes a year or so for the elements to cleanse their nesting-sites. There is a record of an eagle's eyrie in Germany which contained the remains of 300 ducks and 40 hares.

★ 6 ★

PEREGRINES

THE PEREGRINE falcon, *Falco peregrinus* has been in the news a good deal during the past ten years. This is mainly because the bird is considered by a number of ornithologists to be a dwindling species if not one exactly doomed to extinction. Few want to see the peregrine go the way the osprey once went but there are people in this country who could be described as peregrine-haters. These are the lovers of pigeons, and particularly racing pigeons. It must be admitted that there are a great many more people interested in pigeons in Britain than there are concerned about peregrines. I live in pigeon-racing country and I know the almost fanatical love pigeon-racing folk have for their birds. There is hardly a railway station in this neighbourhood which does not have its basket, or baskets, of these racing doves on the platform during the week-end when the contest season is at its height. Recently there was quite an uproar in the press, and on television, about this question of the peregrines predelection for pigeons. Some of the pigeon fraternity maintained that hundreds, if not thousands, of their stock were being taken by these falcons. Proof was said to have been produced in the form of a number of pigeon leg-rings which had been found in pere-grines' eyries. The B.B.C., of course, got into this—it was news —and they put on a show of the pro and anti peregrine factions, just to give the programme the necessary pictorial background they showed a stuffed buzzard in the studio!

The peregrine is, along with most other curved-beak, claw-footed birds, on the protected list in this country but that a few still get shot I have little doubt, but whether shooting is actually a potent factor in the decline of these grand birds I am not sure. It has been suggested that the modern, powerful chemical

compounds with which the farmer is now sousing this country
has contributed towards the peregrines' dwindling. Here again
I find it hard to agree with the anti-chemical-sprayers. The
cause may possibly be a combination of circumstances which is
making this country an uncomfortable place for peregrines.
The pigeon-lover, the chemist, a gradual absorption by man of
natural peregrine terrain, and possibly the over-zealous ornithologist and bird photographer as well, may all, in their
various ways, have contributed to the peregrine's decline. The
latter generally attempt their pictorial efforts during nidification, or more usually brooding, and, I am convinced, disturbance at this period is a sure way to ultimately reduce the
population.

We get records of peregrines having been seen in Northumberland, nearly every year, and occasionally a dead bird comes
into the Hancock Natural History Museum for identification.
At present, as far as I know, we have no pairs nesting there,
although a pair used to nest regularly near the Bezzil Ravine
in the Cheviots and I have seen these birds on more than one
occasion when walking in the Cheviot hills.

I am a lover of the peregrine. I think he is a grand bird far
more romantic in many ways than the soaring golden eagle.
My most exciting experience of peregrines was in Scotland.
For many years I used to stalk red deer stags in an Angus deer
forest in September or October and I also went up to the glen
during the spring, not to shoot, but because it was a very lovely,
restful place simply full of bird-life during the month of May.
Peregrines, in those days, sometimes nested in the steep face
above the well-known Loch Brandy but they eventually went
elsewhere. Perhaps Brandy became too over-run with human
hikers and pony-trekkers. Later peregrines were reported to
have built on the steep face about Loch Whirral which is a
very short flight from Loch Brandy and is far less frequented
by man and horse. Whether these birds still nest by Whirral I
am not certain. They were not there last year. Somewhere,
however, in this vicinity peregrines still linger on and I saw
a pair quite recently up on the top of Ben Tirran from the
summit of which, on a fine day, you can see the smoke of
Dundee.

I was with my stalker and we had had a long, blank morning without seeing a single stag. Towards noon we were on the high tundra-land in sight of Ben Tirran's massive bald pate. The country around was studded with black peat hags some of which had been used recently by the stags and hinds as wallowing places. Patches of deer hair still floated on the glutinous, black ooze, in a number of these mud baths, but of living deer there were none in sight. There were plenty of blue hares though and most of them were remarkably tame. They would freeze to crouch, hunched up, in some peat hag, hoping, I suppose, not to be seen while all the time they were most conspicuous. Perhaps it was this abundant population of hares which attracted the peregrines to this high plateau for Murdo, my stalker, said he often saw the birds about just here.

At one o'clock we decided to have our packed lunch in a dry, sheltered place beneath the lip of a bank of heather.

For one second I thought the bird was a racing pigeon by the rapid wing beat of its flight but then it began to glide and I saw, at once, that it was a peregrine. Another bird now joined the first calling *kek*, *kek*, *kek* in quick succession. In the quiet stillness of the high tundra the voice of the raptore seemed to penetrate everywhere.

Suddenly, one of the pair dropped like a stone to within a foot or so of the earth's surface then, without touching soil, the bird miraculously recovered itself to press on in rapid flight after its mate.

The birds did not seem to want to leave their aerial playground up there on Ben Tirran and they now proceeded to treat me to as fine a display of aerobatics as it has ever been my good fortune to witness.

The peregrines would climb almost vertically and then they would come tumbling down, one milling over the other, whilst, all the time, they kept calling *kwe*, *kwe*, *kwe* with now and again an occasional long-drawn *kee-ack*.

At one stage of their aerial manoeuvres the cock bird did a complete somersault beneath the hen and then climbed up to her to turn on his back and offer her his claws. There, above our heads, the two birds shook hands as it were.

★ 7 ★

OSPREYS

I HAVE NOT had a great deal of personal experience of British ospreys because I live in England and for many years now these birds have not nested here. In the past the osprey used to breed in Devon, Wales and the Lake District but today his efforts at nidification are mainly confined to the Loch Garten district in Scotland. However, I have been able to keep a fairly accurate record of the ospreys who have crossed the Northumbrian coast to visit us, temporarily, since 1950. It is an impressive list as ospreys have been observed every year since 1950 by entirely reliable witnesses, except for the year 1952 when no records were received. One favourite haunt of the ospreys visiting Northumberland has been Gosforth Park which is almost within the precincts of the City of Newcastle. The lake in the park has been their chosen fishing place but as this has recently been partly drained the ospreys may well give it a wide berth in the future. Out of the list of visitors only two died here and neither of these were shot. One was an emaciated, sickly bird which was picked up on May 10th, on whom there were no signs of injury. The other casualty flew into a high-tension electric cable near Cambois. If the Northumbrian coastline were more precipitous than it is, with sufficient vegetation such as is found around the coasts of the Balearic Islands and Sweden then, I think, there would be a fair chance of ospreys staying here to nest.

I saw my first foreign ospreys in Sweden in 1956 when I visited Stockholm and then spent a week-end in June near Ripsa, with Professor Harry von Eckermann and his wife, at their delightful country house at Edeby. On Sunday, after lunch, we took the launch to cruise through the chain of lakes with which the countryside is festooned. The launch was a most comfortable affair glassed-in in front, so that it was possible to keep warm under cover, when travelling at speed which it was necessary to do as we had much water to traverse.

The bird I saw high in the sky, near a tiny rocky islet, looked like a big edition of a kestrel. When I focussed my binoculars on the bird I, at once, noticed the white in its plumage. After hovering for a few seconds the osprey began to plummet downwards towards the surface of the lake. Once he checked himself slightly, in his dive, as if he was trying to make sure that his quarry was still there. He hit the water with a splash which temporarily concealed him from our sight. The osprey rose from the lake with a fish in his talons. It was impossible at the distance to tell its species but Professor von Eckermann said he thought it was most probably a pike as the waters around abound with these fish.

The fishing bird returned with his prey to a nearby rocky islet on which a dozen pine trees grew. This island, together with several others in the locality, was the age-old nesting site of the ospreys of Edeby. All the nests had been built in fir trees and were of massive dimensions. Through my binoculars they looked exactly like the two recent nests of the Loch Garten ospreys.

During nearly the whole of our journey through these Swedish lakes we were in sight of ospreys and many of these birds were still feeding their young in their nests. The place was a scene of constant avian activity. After watching these birds for several hours I knew why they were referred to as fish-eagles for they are certainly superb fishermen. Having read Seton Gordon's remarks that the osprey carries his fish head-first, with one foot in front of the other, I particularly watched for this feature, and it is so, but whether this is done to ensure a greater velocity in the air of the bird and his prey as Seton Gordon suggests I am not sure.

My theory is—and it is only a theory because I have not been able to prove it sufficiently—that the osprey when he actually strikes his prey, beneath the surface of the water, does so with one talon only; then having secured the fish the other leg is instantly brought into action to grasp the fish immediately behind the talon making the first strike.

The year after my visit to Edeby I went, in February, to the island of Mallorca in the Balearic group. The Balearic Islands are favoured by ospreys. The late Captain P. W. Munn, a British naturalist who has done more for the birds of the Balearic Islands than anyone else, made a study of the osprey whilst he was resident in Alcudia. Munn says that the osprey nests in all the islands of the Balearic Group. My first winter in Mallorca I stayed in a little hotel overlooking the shallow bay of Soller. My delight was great when, at lunch on my first day there, two ospreys came to fish the bay which I could see from my table in the dining room. The pair came nearly every day and almost always at exactly the same time, half past one, to perform their superb feats of angling before our eyes. Most of the visitors in the hotel were quite uninterested at the sight of the ospreys. Some of them said they thought they were seagulls. The majority of my fellow guests obviously considered me mad in my affection for these lovely avian anglers.

The drains of the inland town of Soller end up in the river by that name which in turn emits its refuse into the bay of Soller. Mullet are dirty feeders and it is the mullet which is the attraction of the Soller ospreys. Mullet are largely surface feeders and as such they can be easily seen by these fish-hawks and so provide them with ample meals.

Since my first visit to Mallorca I have been back there every February in order to study the birds of the island. I have never failed to see ospreys, whether it was in the great bay of Pollensa in the north of the island, or in the tiny port of Soller.

It has always surprised me that ospreys have continued to breed freely in the Balearic Islands where many people go about with guns. Such birds as thrushes, blackbirds and larks are much sought after by the resident gunners and the smaller pretty birds like the goldfinch and serin are consistently trapped and caged; even the robin is caught but the robin does not last long as a cage-bird being not sufficient of a grain-eater. He must have insects to survive and in a cage he does not get them.

I think there are a number of reasons why the osprey survives in the Balearics; for one thing they are inedible and for another there is a plethora of ideal nesting sites for these birds amongst the many tiny islets which surround the bigger islands. On many of these islets it is impossible for man to land and then there are the sheer, inaccessible cliffs and precipices which are studded with tall conifers all ideal nesting places for ospreys. The truth is that, except at its nest, the osprey is a very difficult bird to shoot. It has been the custom in this country to blame man for the elimination of the osprey as a breeding bird from the British Isles and the modern ornithologist has gone out of his way, in a great many instances, to vilify such keen and obviously sincere naturalists of the past like Charles St. John of Moray and Sir John Colquhoun of Luss. Colquhoun is blamed for the extermination of the last ospreys on Loch Lomond and St. John for having done away with nearly all the other ospreys then residents in Scotland. Colquhoun in his delightful book *The Moor and the Loch* admits with sorrow that as a young man he might have been responsible for a pair of ospreys leaving the old castle of Galbraith on an island in Loch Lomond. He then goes on to say that he was largely influenced by a keeper to shoot the cock and trap the hen.

I sometimes wonder whether these recent attacks on men who are now long dead are entirely justified. I am a great admirer of St. John and having spent a good part of my youth near Elgin I know many parts of the country where St. John practised his natural history, and particularly the lovely Loch of Spynie. Where Captain James Brander Dunbar of Pitgaveny writes me an osprey was recently seen plunging for fish but unfortunately did not stay to breed. In a great many instances both St. John and Colquhoun shot to satisfy their curiosity as did the majority of the best sportsmen naturalists of the past. There is no doubt that we owe a great deal of our present-day knowledge to these men of a departed era who had inquisitive minds. Additionally I cannot see how two men—I know there were others hostile to the osprey as well—could have rid the country of these fish-hawks. That there are suitable, and completely inaccessible, nesting sites for these birds in Britain, I feel sure, just as they are in the Balearics, but possibly not quite so many; and for several years the raptorial birds have had quite a marked degree of protection in this country not necessarily through the law itself but by sentiment as well, and when it comes to sentiment the gunner can be just as sentimental as the non-shooter.

People have often asked me why the osprey thrives and breeds so freely in Sweden whilst it does not do so here. There are, I think, a number of answers to this question. To start with Sweden is a larger and wilder country territorially than is Britain and also it is far less densely populated. There are no breeding ospreys today in Denmark, that I know of, but then Denmark is much more like England and especially the British Islands south of the Scottish Border and east of the Welsh mountains. In agricultural and industrial terrain the osprey appears to be completely out of its element although I believe this does not always apply to some of the overseas species of ospreys such as the American species and certain Middle-Eastern types.

In America the osprey is said to be a community-nester what I saw at Edeby in Sweden was very near communal breeding.

The truth of the matter may well be that the British islands are not desirable nesting places for certain species of birds much as the ornithologist might like to see them here. I am thinking of birds like the erne, or sea-eagle, the osprey, and to a lesser extent the peregrine.

And yet, and in spite of all this, to the joy of the bird-loving interests of this country and the incidental pleasure of a population which is becoming increasingly bird-conscious, the osprey is back. I happened to be in the vicinity of Loch Garten near Nethybridge—I was studying roedeer at the time—when the ospreys appeared and began their preparations to nest in an old nest site, in a fir tree, a few hundred yards from the shores of Loch Garten.

I was watching a pair of roe amongst the marshes on the fringe of the loch when I saw my first British osprey. He or she, I could not tell which, was flying high over the nest. At that moment an authoritative and indignant female voice requested me to get out. I did not. I stayed and was invited into the hide from which the ospreys were being observed and here I became the witness of a most extraordinary episode. Mrs. George Waterston, once she realised that I meant no harm, was very nice indeed. I can well understand her agitation now as when I appeared on the osprey-scene an attempt had just been made scarcely ten minutes previously—to rob the nest of its eggs. George Waterston and two of his male assistants had departed at high speed in a car in an attempt to catch the egg-stealer.

The thief had put the hen bird off the nest and as I could see for myself, with my binoculars, she was still reluctant to settle down. Whilst we were watching a pair of carrion crows came in sight. Crows are amongst the worst of the egg-stealers; it was obvious that they, too, had their eyes on the osprey's eggs. Fortunately at that moment George Waterston and his helpers returned from their unsuccessful attempt to catch the human egg-stealer. Seeing the corbies he immediately instructed his assistants to blow their whistles. Three police whistles now sent their strident screechings across the marshes. The noise had the desired effect for the carrion crows speedily departed. Eventually the ospreys resumed their nesting but tragedy came shortly afterwards for during the hours of darkness the egg-thief came back to make a horrible mess of his stealing for he must have dropped the eggs as they were found broken beneath the nest. There are no words sufficiently strong with which to describe this act of utter vandalism, an act, incidentally which to my mind far surpasses any of the marauding adventures committed by men like St. John and John Colquhoun. For today we should know better.

In 1959 I was back at Nethybridge when the ospreys returned. This time they chose a fresh nesting site not far from the old one. I think one might well be excused for believing that the memory of the previous season's tragedy may have influenced these birds to seek pastures new in which to prepare their nesting arrangements.

The bird protectionists were well organised and out in force and largely due to their vigilance the ospreys nested, laid and successfully brought off their clutch. This gallant attempt on the part of the ospreys to re-establish themselves on our hostile shores has now become national news; the press, the B.B.C. and television are all in on it. Like the Derby, the Grand National and Ascot the annual visit of these fish-hawks has become a seasonal event of national interest and these piscine predators certainly appear to have won the sympathy of the public. Every year thousands of people in cars, on bicycles, in buses, and on foot, go to see the ospreys.

The re-establishment of the osprey as a nesting species in Britain has been well recorded by Philip Brown and George Waterston in their book *The Return of the Osprey*. This was no easy return for time and again the birds were frustrated and usually the offenders were vandals and egg-collectors and not the much vilified keeper and sportsman.

In 1963 I was again staying at Nethybridge when the nest frequented by the ospreys was blown down in a gale. The pair sought quarters elsewhere and on one occasion I was able to watch a fascinating display of nest-building by these displaced ospreys at a rough nest near The Ranch. The ospreys would take off, at regular intervals, from the partially constructed eyrie to make a circle in the woods where there were many dead Scots firs. As a bird passed a dead tree it would snatch a limb in its claw, break it without pausing in its flight, and then carry the piece to the nest where one bird or another, I think it was usually the hen, was ready to receive the timber for her home. Very rarely did an osprey drop a stick and usually these were brought safely to the nest. Some of these branches were formidable branches requiring a good wrench to break them off the parent tree. Although I watched this particular attempt at reconstruction for several evenings running the birds quickly lost interest, presumably to depart elsewhere. For the benefit of the Royal Society for the Protection of Birds who guard so closely the present ospreys' preserves, I should say that all my observations have been made from the safety of the roads so that no trespass has been committed! In 1963 a second pair of ospreys came to Inschriarch, they used an eyrie but nothing happened. Frustration or too much peeking by inquisitive people? Who knows?

The score so far in this series of the U.K. Osprey breeding contests is:

1958   The Year of the Vandals. No hatch.
1959   3 young reared
1960   2 young reared
1961   3 young reared
1962   1 young reared
1963   0 young reared
1964   3 young reared
        —

Total at time of writing   12 Scottish Ospreys
        —

★ 8 ★

OWLS

Owls, perhaps because they are considered to be birds of the night and so do not lend themselves to easy observation, do not appear to have received the publicity that so many other birds have achieved in these days of general ornithological interest. Yet, owls are by no means entirely nocturnal in their habits. Frequently they hunt their prey in broad daylight. I watched a cream-coloured barn owl one day this spring hunting the hedgerows along the main Jedburgh-Newcastle road at three o'clock in the afternoon. The barn owl was most methodical in its questing. It seemed to corkscrew over and around the close-clipped, thorn hedge as if it were searching the roots and the branches for mice or nestling birds. Evidently the hunting was not good for eventually the owl left the road and made towards an irrigation ditch which ran across the adjacent fields. The last I saw of the owl was when it perched itself on the top of a wooden fencing post beside the dyke. If I had not seen it select its perch I would never have known it was there as the barn owl looked a part of the post.

In the month of July, at eleven o'clock in the morning, on the grouse moor of Rhynie in Aberdeenshire, I once watched an unusual gathering of short-eared owls quartering the heather in search of something. I strongly suspect they must have been after grouse chicks as frequently adult grouse would rise from the moor to cackle indignantly at the marauders. The grouses' behaviour reminded me of the false injury trick which so many parent birds practise in an attempt to divert a predator's attention to themselves. I counted fourteen short-eared owls in this hunting pack. Frequently they would perch on the posts by the roadside or on the telegraph poles. The owls took no notice whatever of my car. Although I suspect they were after young grouse for the hatch had been good on Rhynie that year, I must admit I never saw an owl actually pounce to pick its prey.

The commonest owls in this country would appear to be the wood or tawny owl, the barn or screech owl, and in some localities the little owl. The little owl is an import and not an indigenous British bird. It once earned for itself an unenviable reputation as a great killer of little birds as well as the young of gamebirds. Other owls as well as little owls, however, also occasionally take birds as well as insects and rodents. I have often wondered whether the fact that the little owl was originally an imported foreigner has made it unpopular rather than its suspected game-killing habits.

Not so very long ago an owl of any sort was very nearly public enemy number one in the avian world. Not only was the hand of every game-rearer set against him but superstition also dogged his heels so that an owl was a bird to be destroyed. Even today in many countries the owl is still regarded with superstition and is killed whenever possible. Fortunately this does not often happen here, but in parts of Wales the owl is still regarded as a bird of ill-omen. The Jews of North Africa believe the voice of the owl to predict the death of a child and the Arabs regard the presence of an owl as a portent of evil. Every kind of British owl was, at one time, a common sight on the gamekeeper's gallows but now all the owls come within the scope of the Protection of Birds Act of 1954. A great deal of intensive research has been done, prior to the owls' general protection, by various ornithological interests into the diet of owls. This was not an entirely difficult task because of the owl's habit of ejecting the indigestible parts of his food in the form of pellets— an extensive investigation of the pellets of the various owls largely established the fact that most owls fed mainly on the smaller rodents and insects and not to any great extent on the so-called game birds. The combination of protection plus a marked decrease in the keeper population and a greater appreciation, on the part of the public, of these birds has undoubtedly been the cause of an increase in their numbers, at least that is my experience in so far as Northumberland is con-

cerned and I think that this state of affairs is also prevalent
throughout Britain today.

The barn, or screech-owl, because of its partiality to human
habitations is, perhaps, the best-known species to the general
public. Barn owls breed in farm buildings, church towers, ruins
and such-like places. Many towns and villages have their
resident barn owls. Their voices are familiar sounds in the
gloaming and during the hours of darkness. The vocabulary of
these owls is quite astonishing in its immense variety. These
birds can imitate the yowling of a lovelorn cat, they can produce
a near-human shriek and they can chatter and hoot as well as
hiss, snore and yap. During the breeding season they appear to
be particularly vocal and on many an occasion I have lain in
my bed and enjoyed the medley indulged in by our pair of
village barn owls. The flight of the barn owl, like that of most of
the owls, is almost soundless and it is a common enough sight,
today, to see one of these ghostly birds in the headlights of one's
car as the owl glides along the aisles of a country road. The
main intake of the barn owl consists of house sparrows, mice,
voles and rats, however, due to the efficient destruction of rats
by poison and gas this latter item of its menu may well be far
less than it was in the past.

The late George Bolam, of Berwick-on-Tweed, who was an
extremely observant naturalist, believed that at certain times a
considerable number of barn owls visited these shores from
abroad. He observed that periodically, in the past, the local
taxidermists were inundated with numbers of dead barn owls
to be stuffed. These periodic inundations, he suggested, were
the result of an influx of barn owls into this country from overseas. Even today stuffed barn owls are often to be seen in old
cottages, public houses and such-like places. It is an intriguing
theory this that the extent of a particular bird's migration
should be based on evidence of this kind but I believe that
Bolam may well have been right in his view that barn owls do,
at times, arrive in considerable numbers along our eastern
coastal counties.

Several naturalists have suggested that barn owls, and other
owls as well, will carry their young from place to place. This is
said to be done by the owl clutching its chick gently in its

curved talons and not between its thighs as is done in the case of the woodcock. I have never seen an owl air-lift its young but I have seen a woodcock do so as is described elsewhere in this book.

Some of our local barn owls are near-white in colour and the lightness of their plumage is particularly noticeable in the dusk or in a poor light. This whiteness is often inclined to exaggerate the size of the bird and in the fading light of a December afternoon I once saw a great white bird come gliding down a ride through a fir plantation towards where I stood beneath a larch tree. Like most amateur ornithologists I am always hopeful that I may be able to record one of the rarer avian visitors to our shores. I must admit that my thoughts on this occasion turned towards the rare, great snowy owl which is surely the most romantic of all the owls. The bird I saw was, in fact, a light variety of the common barn owl but my wishful thinking was not entirely foolish as the snowy owl has actually visited Northumberland and there are stuffed specimens of these birds in the Hancock Museum in Newcastle upon Tyne. One of these specimens is that of a snowy owl which was shot near Rothbury on the river Coquet not very far from where I live.

Next to the barn owl the wood, or tawny owl, is probably the commonest of the owls up here in the north. It is possible that the wood owl is even more numerous today than the barn owl because so much of the far northern counties of England have now become afforested places thus providing an abundance of the natural habitat of this woodland species of owl.

Of recent years I have had the nesting sites of two pairs of wood owls under close observation in a wood of mixed hardwood and conifers within half a mile of my house. The tawny owl, which is sometimes known as the wood owl or the brown owl, nests like so many of the *Strygidae* in the old nests of crows, wood-pigeons, jackdaws, and magpies. It will also adopt a disused squirrel's drey or a hole in an old tree. In fact, owls are not at all particular about their nesting sites and they are not usually expert architects in the construction of a nest. Any old thing seems to do. My two neighbouring pairs of wood owls have both selected holes in old conifers as their chosen breeding places. Tawny owls, once you have sighted them, are not difficult birds to approach. They frequently sit close to the trunk of a tree and appear then to be quite oblivious to one's presence in their immediate neighbourhood. Actually they are, perhaps, aware of one's proximity but they may well rely on their likeness to their immediate surroundings in an attempt to avoid detection. If, once having spotted an owl, you stand quite still you will see that by screwing his head from side to side the bird will carefully watch your every movement. The owls seem to have a head on their shoulders which can pivot almost right around the central vertebrae. The tawny owl is reputed to be a mainly nocturnal bird but I have seen them abroad in broad daylight on many occasions. Tawny owls can be almost as vocal as their relatives the barn owls. In the past tawny owls were usually shot on sight by both gamekeepers and sportsmen but nowadays it is a rare occurrence for anyone to have a go with a gun at an owl should it appear in a drive or a covert shoot.

The tawny owl is regarded as a non-migratory bird but that they do move about a good deal I have little doubt. Two recent recoveries of tawny owls ringed at Monk's House Bird Observatory at Seahouses were made at Dumfries and Perth. The latter recovery shows an almost direct northerly route of over 100 miles.

As has already been mentioned the little owl is an introduced foreign species and no single person was responsible for its immigration into this country. A variety of naturalists over a period of years would appear to have brought numbers of these birds to Britain. Waterston, Meade-Waldo, Rothschild and Lord Lilford have all been introducers of little owls. Some of these birds came from as far afield as Italy whilst others were of Dutch origin.

At one period the little owl was almost universally proscribed. A keeper or sportsman who would not shoot one of these birds on sight would have been a rarity. The situation now is quite different for the little owl has now been largely exculpated of its alleged addiction to game destruction. Like many of the other species of larger owls the little owl seems to exist quite happily on insects, reptiles, rodents and worms although, undoubtedly, this little bird of catholic tastes will on occasion take a succulent nestling or a fledgling chick.

Little owls have increased in this country and have extended their range into Scotland. Of recent years I have had three separate pairs of little owls under observation within a radius of two miles from this house. One pair—the first observed in the locality—nest in an old elm by the side of the Morpeth-Kirkley road, the pair to the north-east also have their residence in a big tree in a hedgerow. The last pair have nested beneath a road-arch over the infrequently used Morpeth-Rothbury railway. I find little owls fascinating birds to watch with their wood-pecker-like flight and apparent fearlessness of man's immediate presence whilst occupied searching for their food in daylight.

For a long time I was under the erroneous impression that the little owl was the smallest of the owls. I was quite wrong for both the pygmy and scops owls are smaller than the little owl. I have never seen a pygmy owl but for many days I searched for a pair of scops who frequented a garden near where I was staying in Mallorca. The scops has a very distinctive call which once heard it is not easy to forget for it consists of a sort of melancholy whistle. Scops are strictly nocturnal birds and are about the size of a fieldfare so that perhaps it was not altogether surprising that I was unable to get a glimpse of the scops.

The short-eared owl is by no means rare, up here in the border counties, and at certain times of year it is a common sight to see one of these owls, or even a party of them, hunting the moorlands or young conifer plantations. The short-eared owl is a frequent daylight hunter and a very efficient exterminator of voles and mice. There would appear to be a definite correlation between the numbers of voles and the presence of short-eared owls for a plague of voles will generally be accompanied by a corresponding increase in the number of short-eared owls. George Bolam has suggested that the immigrant short-eared owls may well be daylight hunters because in the far northern latitudes, where these birds are numerous, the sun during the summer months never sets so that daylight lasts during the whole 24 hours and to feed at all these owls have to secure their prey in broad daylight.

Short-eared owls are both a resident and a migratory species in the northern counties. There seems to be a regular influx of these birds from across the North Sea in the autumn and a corresponding departure from these shores in the early spring.

The long-eared owl is also both a resident and a visitor from overseas to Britain but because the long-eared owl is more of a nocturnal bird than his near cousin the short-eared owl he is not so frequently observed. According to Bannerman & Lodge no British ringed long-eared owls have been accounted for from overseas *but* ringed Swedish, Dutch and German birds have been recovered in this country. Long-eared owls appear to have a preference for coniferous woods and pairs of these birds were not infrequently to be found in the old coniferous wind-brakes and sheep-shelters which abound in the northern counties. Today with the extensive planting of vast soft-wood forests such as Kielder, Wark, Newcastleton, Harwood and Thrunton one may well be permitted to assume that these owls are now more numerous in northern Britain than they have ever been before.

★ 9 ★

WOODCOCK

THE WOODCOCK is a favourite bird of mine as it is of many others who are interested in birds. I know woodcock-admirers in Spain, France, Belgium and Germany not to mention this country. The woodcock is a very interesting character; even his scientific name of *Scolopax rusticola* seems to me to have a ring of the romantic about it.

I cannot think of any other so-called sporting bird who is able to create such a furore by his sudden presence at a covert shoot.

Woodcock, because they have a habit of turning up suddenly in unexpected places, very frequently provide the sportsman with the surprise packet of his day's shooting.

We now know that at certain times of the year woodcock come to this country and go away again very quickly. No set, or organised, attempt to pre-arrange a woodcock shoot, as such, can ever hope to be a certain success for the birds are often here today and gone tomorrow. On one occasion when shooting a tiny strip of larch, beside the A.1 road south of Alnwick in Northumberland—it was certainly under two acres in extent— the beaters put up over 30 woodcock. This means, of course, that there must have been many more birds in the vicinity which we never saw.

The habit the woodcock has of arriving in a place to depart again quickly for some distance destination makes an accurate assessment of the 'cocks' influx in any particular area a complete impossibility—all we can hope to do is guess at figures. Woodcock are said to come over the North Sea to us, in a south-westerly drift, from the Scandinavian countries during the late autumnal and early winter moon periods, but their travelling schedule has, by no means, been fully proven. Some observers believe that misty weather is a favourable condition for the flighting of the 'cock. At the same time others prefer to regard a clear moonlight night as the woodcocks' ideal travelling weather. The truth is that we are likely to have both conditions in an average November—but the fact that November, in this country, can over a period of years provide many days of mist and fog may have influenced people, interested in bird migration, to pitch for the foggy-night theory. Whenever and however they come, once arrived here, local weather conditions, I am sure, then, immediately begin to control their temporary residence, within a particular area, or their immediate departure. A nice sunny spell in November will hold 'cock for a while to a particular place. Cold, hard, frosty weather will send them on to more hospitable climes like southern Ireland and the western lowlands of France.

Today, I am quite convinced, that there are more of these birds nesting with us here in the far north of England than there were fifty years ago. For one thing the conditions for the woodcocks' permanent residence here are, nowadays, much more favourable than they have been in the past. A great area of the northern English counties of Northumberland, Durham, Cumberland and Westmorland is now afforested and much of these young woodlands make good 'cock covers.

Further, since 1954 the woodcock has been granted a longer close-season, during which he may not be shot. Today the "cease-fire" at woodcock begins at dawn on February 1st whereas previously he was regarded, in most counties where local orders governed his protection under the Wild Birds Protection Acts, as a fair target up and until the last day of February.

The woodcock is an early-nester and before ever nidification takes place—and nidification is usually a very sketchy affair when it comes to woodcock—quiet is required and not constant disturbance during the pre-nuptial period. Constant disturbance of the birds' haunts, during this time, will quickly drive them away. The new close-season gives the 'cock a better chance to stay and breed.

As an instance of early breeding a letter in *The Field* of April 7th, 1960, is interesting. Mr. Carnegy-Arbuthnot of Balnamoon, Brechin, Angus, reports that his keeper N. Cleghorn watched a woodcock carrying its young on March 9th. Although this may seem an abnormally early date for breeding it does indicate that the close-season now in force for woodcock is, by no means, too generous.

Until comparatively recently woodcock appear to have been shot during every month of the year and not only during the early spring months. The Reverend F. O. Morris, to quote him once again, gives instances of this happening. This may have been due to the fact that at one time 'cock were regarded as almost entirely migratory birds and not permanent residents. There is still a strong belief amongst the shooting fraternity that to shoot visitants is quite harmless and that to have to put one's shot-gun in its case or cupboard, for a period, is only necessary *pro bono* the local nesting species.

During the past twenty-five years one of my main outdoor preoccupations has been the study of that delightful animal the graceful roedeer. These creatures are mostly active during dawn and dusk periods which are also largely favoured by the woodcock for his feeding and "roding". The "roding", or display activity of these birds, is an extremely entertaining and interesting performance. It takes place, I think, more frequently in the gloaming than at day-break although this admittedly is only the experience of one individual. The sound made by the "roding" 'cock, as they fly along the rides, or in the glades of a wood, is quite extraordinary—it is rather like an exaggerated grunt a sort of *awk*.

Woodcock appear to return to the same place, or somewhere quite close to it, every year to nest—provided that the terrain has not been too much altered, in the interregnum between nesting periods, or that the birds are not unduly disturbed. For the past three years I have noticed two pairs of woodcocks who have selected for their breeding sites the same spots in a mixed wood of oak and scattered conifers within a mile of the house I live in.

It is now an accepted fact in ornithological circles that woodcock can carry their young ones. I saw this happen during the dawn on one occasion near the Moray Firth and I have described this episode elsewhere in this book. However, there is still argument as to exactly how this infant-portage is conducted. Does the adult bird gather its young in its feet or between the thighs? I believe the carrier squats above her offspring to gather it in her thighs, above the knee joints, but other observers have stated that the parent's feet are used to grasp the young bird and that sometimes a woodcock will fly with her chick held around the neck in her claws. The whole subject of avian infant-portage is one that could do with a great deal more investigation; to me, at least, it is a fascinating problem and one well worth spending much time on.

The mounted fox-hunter frequently has far better opportunities of noticing "falls" of 'cock—that is their arrival in numbers in a particular place—than has the more static shooter or bird-watcher. For one thing a hunt covers, in the space of a day, a vastly greater area than a pedestrian can. A pack of hounds hunting, spread out, through a cover or moorland will certainly set on wing as many birds, or even more, than a line of beaters. I have frequently noticed a fresh "fall" of 'cock in a certain locality when out with hounds. A day or two later when over the same ground, once again with hounds, not a single cock will be flushed. By far the biggest congregation of woodcock I have ever seen was not really a proper "fall" of 'cock at all. During the long, hard winter of 1947 the ground inland became largely icebound for months on end. The long-billed inland waders suffered considerably simply because they could not get their beaks into the earth to feed. It was during this period that large numbers of 'cock packed along the coast-line and the sand dunes adjoining the sea. The tidal stretches were about the only unfrozen areas in the district and thousands of all sorts of birds collected in these zones to pick up what they could. Many hundreds of birds died of starvation and amongst them great numbers of woodcock. Walking along the dunes it was quite possible to pick up woodcock because they could only fly a very short distance. It was a tragic sight, one I shall never forget. One bird I picked up had a breast bone on it like a knife. I scarcely knew whether to put it down again, after I had taken it up to examine it, or to wring its neck—I put it down. Perhaps it would have been kinder to release it quickly from a slow death through starvation.

In 1962 I was so fortunate as to witness, at close range, a strange performance between two woodcocks. It was just after one o'clock on a cold day in May. The wind, accompanied by rain and sleet, which fell as snow on the Cairngorms was coming from the north-east. I walked over the hill of Ord Bain into a little moss-covered glade, studded with a number of silver birches. A doe roedeer barked when she got a touch of my wind. Suddenly between the white trunks of the birch trees I saw two dark-brown lumps leap into the air. Fortunately I had my binoculars with me and focussing them on the spot where the lumps had sprung from I saw, to my astonishment, two woodcocks who appeared to be engaged in some sort of dance. The birds would face each other whilst squatting on the ground and then suddenly leap into the air like acrobatic jumpers. When they did this they seemed to lean backwards whilst, at the same time, they extended their feet towards each other in just the way I have seen gamecocks perform when fighting in the cockpits of Spain.

Now and again the pair of birds would settle on the soft, mossy terrain to circle one another until one of the cocks tried to spring on top of the other. Sometimes one of the woodcocks would strut with its wings trailing as blackgrouse do when they are engaged on the *lek*. I watched the pair, in fascination, standing within ten yards of the birds for at least five minutes. That they never saw me I am convinced for one of them, whilst circling the other, came to within a few feet of where I stood. Suddenly one of the 'cocks took off to fly low over the ground towards the pine woods on the shore of Loch-an-Eilan. Its companion almost immediately sprang into flight to follow. The last I saw of the pair they were chasing one another through the scattered conifers within sight of the little island in the loch where the ospreys used to nest.

Whilst this display was going on the two birds were silent except for a slight gutteral noise which I heard the bird nearest to me make when it pitched almost at my feet. The voice of the 'cock sounded as if it came from deep down in the throat.

It certainly did not resemble the note a woodcock utters when it is engaged on its *roding* flights.

The scene I had observed that day in May may have been a sort of mating dance leading up to a second nest as these birds are known to have two clutches in a season and exceptionally even three.

★ 10 ★

CURLEWS

I HAVE A friend who has a small farm on the fringe of the Simonside hills. He is over 80 years of age and he started farming long before the subsidies. His has been a hard life but he seems to have thoroughly enjoyed it. His passion is foxhunting and any vixen desirous of accommodation on his place during the period of her confinement is very welcome. I have never known Jim's farm without a litter or two of fox cubs on it.

Jim is well versed in the ways of the wild and his knowledge of both birds and beasts is encyclopaedic although he is the first to admit that he is in no sense a learned scientist. One recent winter Jim was very ill and there was some doubt as to whether he would see the spring. I saw him soon after he recovered and he said:

"When I heard the curlew come, towards the end of February, I knew I would live."

The call of the curlew is to those who live near the high moors the first welcome sound that winter is on its way out. The voice of these curved bill waders is a sound to charm the least musical of us. To me it is one of the most beautiful tunes in the world. Soon after curlews come the wheatears appear but they arrive from much further away for most of our upland nesting curlews move up from the sea to their territories in the hills in February and March. However, Abel Chapman has stated in his book *Bird Life of the Borders* that our nesting birds are from overseas whereas our coastal curlews go further north to nest. This fact, nevertheless, has never been satisfactorily proved.

Blackcocks *lek* on Jim's hill farm and there is a permanent badgers' sett in the ghyll below the greystone farm house. It is a very lively place in the spring.

The cock curlews are the first to arrive on Jim's hill farm where they establish their territories. Jim claims to know the individual birds by some peculiar trait or colouring. He says the birds always come to their old territories and unless one dies, or is killed, the pair are always the same. How he can tell I do not know but that he is convinced of this fact there is no doubt.

Sometimes a bird will arrive prematurely to be greeted by ice and snow, the tailend of a bitter winter, but he will persist and rarely does he return to the lowlands in spite of the inclement highground weather. Curlews are known to have nested up as high as 2000 feet. Once established the hens come to their chosen cocks and then begins a fantastic display of aerial gymnastics accompanied by ecstatic song.

Flying low over the rough, yellow grass a cock will suddenly climb with quick strokes of his wings. Having reached altitude he then puts on all his air-brakes, as it were, to stall and then he flutters, in a kestrel-like manner, before breaking into a thrilling repeated cry of *coorlee, coorlee, coorlee*. The cadence of the song increases to a quick tempo which becomes almost a trill when the volume sweeps over hill and dale telling all that spring has come. After the first outburst the cock dips almost to the earth's surface and then ascends again to sing once more.

Most of the pre-nuptial display appears to take place in the air but I have seen a cock put on a ruff-like performance before his hen. It happened on Jim's farm. The hen was squatting as if she was already brooding her eggs which she was not as she had not laid as yet. The cock began to walk around her in ever tightening circles and then suddenly he puts on a most delightful dance which reminded me of a sort of avian ballet. With wings raised and outstretched the cock now fluttered his primaries as he walked around his beloved.

The hens start to lay about the end of April. Their nests are scrappy affairs and sometimes merely a little scrape on the rough ground. Four eggs would appear to be the normal complement and although these are quite well camouflaged I am sure a lot are stolen by that vastly greedy egg-eater the carrion crow. Carrion crows are certainly the curlew's worst enemy, and some of the aerial combats, I have witnessed, between these two species were marvellous spectacles. Once spotted, however, by a carrion crow a curlew's clutch has not much of a chance of survival for this black marauder is a very persistent bird.

The incubation period of the curlew is about a month and both parents share in the duty of sitting on the eggs. Young curlews, lovely downy bundles, are precocious but not so nimble on the leg as either young pheasants or partridges when first hatched.

Families stick close together even when the young are fledged and able to fly good distances. With the coming of August wanderlust takes over the curlews. The family parties, now all well on the wing, head for the sea and once again the evening August sky is filled with the travelling song of the returning birds. It is a near melancholy sound this good-bye dirge as the curlews pass high overhead sometimes above cloud level and often in the darkening. In September the families pack to form flocks of thirty to fifty birds and they often remain in these gatherings until the spring break-up again. Curlews would seem to migrate from east to west in the fall of the year as far as Ireland and sometimes further still, and then they fly back again in the spring when they leave their communities to make the journey into the uplands for the purposes of pro-creation.

Quite a lot of curlews, however, appear all through the winter months on the Northumbrian coast and it is no unusual sight to see anything from a dozen to sixty birds on the seashore searching for crabs, mussels and other molluscs amongst the rock pools and tangled seaweed.

Some curlews live to a considerable age and there is a record in volume nine of David Armitage Bannerman's *The Birds of the British Isles* of a curlew, ringed at Vastland, Sweden in 1926, which was eventually recovered thirty-two years later in 1958 at Blakeney in Norfolk, surely a remarkable instance of longevity—not far short in avian senescence to Jim's eighty years.

★ 11 ★

RAVENS

I HAD GONE up to Harbottle Moor—which is a part of the Cheviot range of hills—to see how the red grouse had fared after their nesting season. Reaching the northern march of the moor at mid-day, I ate my sandwiches by the Barrow Burn and then stretched out in the thick heather to enjoy a pipe.

It was one of those warm, lovely days in late June, when summer seems finally to have come to the high Northumberland moors. A light westerly breeze blew the infrequent cloud wisps towards the bald peak of old Cheviot. The silence of the moor was impressive.

Suddenly, a distant sound broke the stillness. It was the deep, throaty *cronk, cronk* of a hunting raven. Searching the sky with my binoculars I picked up two tiny black specks in the blue vault above. I could hardly believe, for a moment, that the sound had come from such a distance. I guessed that the birds were not far below ten thousand feet. That ravens do climb to immense heights is well known, as is the fact that their voices have extreme powers of penetration, but my first experience of these facts was exciting.

I have come across ravens when in the Swiss Alps at heights of over 10,000 feet. There is a record of a raven having visited one of the camps of the 1951 Everest expedition at an elevation of 21,000 feet. Ravens are to be found in many parts of the world and in places as far apart as the Himalayas, the Canary Islands, Finland, the Caucasus, Arabia, Persia and the British Isles. Although many of the ravens of different parts of the world have been granted sub-specific status a number of ornithologists regard the ravens of these various countries as belonging to a single species.

Although I had never seen ravens before on Harbottle Moor,

I knew that pairs were in the habit of nesting in the Bezzil ravine, which lies at the back of the Cheviots. It would be no achievement for them to have come visiting us, situated but seven miles to the south of the Bezzil.

The ravens' nesting sites in this dark corrie, which runs from the north into the hills, are frequently in the face of the precipice which falls sheer from the rim of the ravine to its bottom. The sun, even in mid-summer, seldom reaches the foot of this dour cleft.

Ravens are reputed to mate for life, although, if one of a pair is killed, the bereft one is often quickly consoled by the arrival of a new suitor.

The nest, or fortress, of the raven is seldom built in the same spot twice. Each year a fresh site is selected by the breeding pair. The belief is that hygiene compels them to do this. As carrion feeders, the homes in which they breed and raise their young quickly become nauseating spots, giving out a powerful stench, as anyone knows who has looked down into a raven's fortress with the wind blowing upwards into his face. Although the majority of ravens in the British Isles now build their nests on crags, cliffs and precipices, at one time, when these birds were more numerous than they are today, they frequently built their fortresses in trees. Last spring in a hidden ghyll, behind Southernknowe, in the College Valley, I came across the nest of a pair of ravens with three fledglings in it. This nest had been built in a big elm growing in the course of a tiny burn. I was able to obtain an excellent photograph of this raven's fortress.

The raven, the largest of our British crows, has a wing span of well over four feet. It is not so much their size, however, which is impressive but rather the power and strength of their massive beaks. These they use to rend their victims and sometimes before they are dead.

When the weather is wild and gales blow over Cheviot, the ravens may be seen zooming and diving in the boisterous winds. They certainly give one the impression that they are enjoying themselves. It is this habit of theirs which has earned them the reputation of being birds of wild weather.

In some parts of the country the appearance of a raven is considered an omen of ill, and particularly is this the case of some localities in Scotland. I remember one day when I was stalking red deer in the forest of Rothiemurchus. I had spied a stag well above me on the hillside. It was not a difficult stalk. I had got within shot of the stag when I felt a tug on my sleeve from the stalker who lay beside me. As he pointed towards the sky I heard the familiar *cronk*, *cronk* of a raven.

"Ye'll no miss yon staag noo", I heard my companion whisper. As we went in to gralloch the dead stag, I asked my stalker why he was so certain of my shooting as I am normally a somewhat mediocre performer with a rifle. He replied with complete conviction that the presence of the ravens above indicated that a deer would shortly die.

Some years ago when I was staying in the little fishing village of Soller in the island of Mallorca I had taken a walk along the path beneath the old watch-tower to the north of the port. Suddenly a pair of ravens came past me in a steep dive uttering their penetrating calls as they tumbled downwards towards the sea eight hundred feet below. The birds disappeared from my sight. When I returned, later in the morning, to the harbour I found a tragedy had occurred. A young English boy had gone out fishing along the steep cliff side beneath the watch-tower. He had fallen and broken his leg. He had lain there amongst the rocks unable to move. Two fishermen in a motor vessel were on their way back to Soller when they noticed two ravens circling above the rocks where the boy lay incapacitated. Curious as to the birds behaviour the fishermen chanced to locate the youth. They were able to reach the boy and bring him back to port. This is the kind of incident which has earned for the raven his reputation as a bird of disaster, although in this particular case if it had not been for the presence of this pair of ravens it might well have been a considerable time before this accident came to be discovered. These Mallorcan ravens, by their vulturine behaviour, may well, in fact, have saved the boy's life.

During the 1939–45 war the ravens of the Tower of London nearly became extinct. There is a tradition that when the ravens desert the Tower, the White Tower will fall and, with it, the British Empire. Immediate steps were taken to re-establish these birds within the precincts of the Tower. Four nestlings were brought from the far north of Scotland and two from the mountains of Wales. All these fledglings had their wings clipped to prevent their escape. They quickly settled in their new home as ravens adapt themselves rapidly to captivity. The Scottish birds took up their residence by the Leathorn Tower, whilst the Welsh established their domain by Tower Green.

Occasionally "Cronk", one of the male Scots, used to penetrate the territory of the Welsh, but he was always repulsed for his temerity and driven home to his own domain. I have always regretted that one, or two, of our Border birds from the Bezzil were not also introduced to the Tower at the same time as the Welshmen and Scotsmen. If this had been done, I have no doubt that Border warfare between the Scots and the English, within the precincts of the Tower of London, would have been revived!

★ 12 ★

THE CORVINE
MENACE

ANYONE WISHING to make a generic study of birds might do a lot worse than select the corvidae who are the largest members of the passerines or perching birds. For one thing there are not too many different kinds of crow and some species are very numerous. Others like the jackdaw can be quite tame and so easy to study.

The crow family, in this country, consists of the raven, the two carrion crows, the hooded and the black, the rook, the jackdaw, the magpie, the jay and the somewhat scarcer chough. There are other European crows like the azure winged magpie, the Siberian jay and the Alpine chough but these need not be taken into account for they rarely, if ever, visit these shores.

In a lot of ways crows are fascinating birds and although most of them are common there would still seem to be a good deal to be learnt about them.

There has undoubtedly been a considerable increase in the corvine population since the outbreak of the second world war in 1939. I mention this year because it was then that the shortage of gamekeepers in this country became really acute. The war undoubtedly gave these carrion birds a wonderful opportunity to build up their numbers, further, by 1939 a good part of this country was already quite well afforested since the Forestry Commission started their career in 1919. Timber seems to be almost an essential for the majority of crows although the raven, the jackdaw and the chough appear to be able to do quite well without trees.

I do not think there is much doubt that the gamekeeper was

probably the most potent control factor on the population of the less desirable corvidae like the carrion crow, the hooded crow, the magpie and to a lesser extent the jay.

Another factor was certainly the pole trap, a cruel device, but a most effective one when used with skill against perching birds. The pole trap is now an illegal instrument and severe penalties may result if it is used.

Poison, and particularly strychnine, was another powerful weapon in the control of undesirable carrion feeders and nest destructors. The efficient use of strychnine must have accounted for far more hooded and carrion crows than any amount of shooting or trapping. Strychnine, a deadly poison, should only be used under the strictest of controls. One trouble about strychnine is that it lingers. I heard of a case where a fox killed with strychnine was buried, some ten years later it was, for some reason, unearthed and a carrion crow messing about with the remains was killed. Strychnine is still used but nothing like to the extent it once was. There have been some terrible tragedies with this most deadly of poisons.

Extensive re-afforestation, throughout the length and breadth of Britain, has undoubtedly provided fine shelter for crows, magpies and jays. As these birds are all generally harmless to arboriculture they are not interfered with, to any degree, by the forester.

The increase in the corvine population is not confined to any one part of the British Isles. It appears to be universal. In some parts of the country, however, the growth in numbers appears to be more marked than in others. On the whole the increase in the numbers of these birds is not by any means a good thing, in fact, in many instances it is a thoroughly bad one.

Admittedly, the shooting man is in the minority in Britain and the eggs and young of game birds the crow family destroys do not matter much to the bulk of the human population of these islands *but* crows are not selective they will steal the eggs and chicks of garden birds and other harmless avians. The raven, written about elsewhere in this book, is the largest member of the corvine family and he is now almost a rare bird although I think that ravens, on the whole, have increased slightly in their numbers over the past ten years. They have certainly not become so numerous as to become a menace, as they might well have done, for the raven can be just as bad a hat as the hoodie or the carrion crow. Now that the raven seems to be adequately controlled in numbers he should be kept where he is.

All the crow family seem to have a very strong streak of wiliness in their make-up and particularly the magpie, jay and the two crows. Once any of these birds realise that man is an enemy it takes a lot to get them. They seem to know instinctively the effective range of a shotgun.

During the last few years, in the north of England and parts of eastern Scotland, the menace of the carrion crow has become so acute that the agricultural authorities, in the form of the local branches of the Ministry of Agriculture and Fisheries, have stepped in and taken an active part in dealing with these destructive birds. Crow-shoots have been arranged during the early months of the year. These battues are conducted at, or near, the known communal roosting places of these birds.

Shooting usually commences before dusk and if a night of full moon is chosen the crows, coming into their habitual perching places, may be destroyed well after dark as the black birds can be clearly seen in silhouette against a moonlit sky.

It is, perhaps, a little surprising that these great, communal gatherings of both the carrion and hooded crows have not been more generally commented on by ornithologists before. In the comparatively recent past, both the hooded and carrion crow, have been largely regarded as somewhat solitary birds living a paired life. It is surely possible that the present communal gatherings of these birds, at certain times of the year, are a result of their enormous increase.

Carrion and hooded crows are not yet, as far as I know, communal nesters, like the rooks, in this country, although I have noticed recently, in my immediate neighbourhood, quite a few crows' nests built pretty close together.

Next to the carrion crow and the hooded crow, whom some ornithologists regard as conspecific, magpies have increased more than any of the other corvidae. The "maggie" was a comparatively rare bird in a great many parts of this country prior to the 1939–45 war. There is little doubt that the outlawing of the lethal post-trap has acted very much in the magpie's favour. It is not so easy to shoot a magpie as it is to kill a crow, rook, or jackdaw, with a gun. Gamebird preservers usually go for a magpie's nest as a possible seat of future magpie population. But a shot from a twelve-bore gun will make little impression on the oval fortresses which are these birds' nests. An attempt to break up a magpie's nest is an arduous business, seldom entirely successful as "maggie" often comes back to build again.

Motoring about the country today one sees almost as many of these birds as one does on the Continent of Europe where the magpie has a sort of magic protection about him which enables him to live and maraud farms, chicken runs, and the nests of thousands of the lesser avian fry.

I do not think that jays have multiplied quite as much as magpies. That jays have increased in numbers, there is no doubt. The jay is an entirely woodland bird, and with the very considerable increase we have seen, in this country, in woodland acreage any potential augmentation of the jay population has had ample territory in which to multiply. Jays can be merciless butchers and once accepted in a garden they can play havoc with the local, little-bird population. Both eggs and fledglings are fair game to *Garrulus glandarius* the somewhat glamorous generic name under which the jay bird squawks.

Jackdaws have not only increased appreciably in numbers, during recent years, but they also appear to have learnt some nasty tricks. Jackdaws, like most of the crow family, appear to have a liking for the eggs of other birds and even their nestlings. A local jackdaw recently invaded a hen run to pick up a chick and take off with it. Historically, the jackdaw has been accused of seeing off the rare chough from a number of localities. This, I think, is possibly due to the fact that both choughs and jackdaws like rocky cliffs in which to nest. The jackdaw being the stronger bird probably ousted the smaller chough from its habitual nesting sites.

Rooks too are learning some very bad habits but because they are considered to be mainly insectivorous they are largely tolerated.

During the lambing season, in March this year, I happened

to come across a ewe with two still-born lambs beside her. Two black birds were already on the scene of the birth and were engaged in tackling the warm remains of the twin lambs. I was a little surprised when I saw the birds were rooks and not carrion crows as I expected. A good deal has been written about so-called rook parliaments when a gathering of these birds surround a solitary member, evidently condemn him after a good deal of cawing, and then proceed to execute him. That such things happen there seems little doubt and I believe that it is not only rooks who hold these judgements but also jackdaws and possibly carrion crows as well.

Nowadays, early in the year, one often sees considerable collections of carrion crows numbering as many as forty birds. It is during these congregations that the executions take place.

By the end of March the carrioneers break up into pairs to start their individual nests and they appear to stay *au pair*, or with the family they raise, until winter comes once more.

13

SEA GULLS AND
OTHERS

ONCE I DID a dreadful thing; I have never forgiven myself for it, I put out a night-line across a tidal stretch of the river Lossie in the hope of getting a dish of dabs for breakfast. All I caught was a line of herring gulls. When I arrived early in the dawn to pull in my line I found a sea gull on nearly every hook. I was horrified at the unwitting cruelty of my act. Fortunately I had with me a .22 magazine rifle. With it I dispatched the captive gulls as speedily as possible. When I handled the dead birds I remembered being astonished at the beauty of their plumage. Since then I am glad to say that I have never killed a gull.

During the last war I had to go on a course at Balliol, Oxford. In Brown's, the famous booksellers opposite the Bodelian, I discovered a folder full of original water-colour paintings by Henrik Grönvold, amongst these pictures was one of a herring gull in gliding flight. It is one of the most realistic paintings of birds I have ever seen. It is the more unusual as most of Grönvold's work is of the static kind. Grönvold worked for a number of years in the Natural History Museum in Kensington. He was responsible for illustrating a number of books on birds. The painting of the herring gull now hangs on the wall of my study. I never fail to get great pleasure from it. Several people have mistaken this water-colour for a photograph.

I often wonder whether the presence of this picture did not subconsciously influence me to take a special interest in the gulls.

At one time I thought I would never be able to sort out the

various kinds, although as far as Britain is concerned there are not, by any means, a great number of varieties, provided that we exclude such comparatively rare visitors as some of the arctic gulls and the mediterranean birds.

I decided to confine my interest to the great black-back, the lesser black-back, the herring, the common, the black-headed gulls and the kittiwake. The fulmar although in many respects a remarkable gull-like bird is not a gull at all but a tubenose which is now the more favoured name for a petrel. Fortunately I live within range of some of the fulmar's nesting places in this country so that I have also had unlimited opportunities of observing this most intriguing pelagic bird, perhaps one of the world's greatest natural gliding experts. The kittiwake also an oceanic species nests nearby on the Farne Islands, Dunstanburgh, North Shields and Marsden Rock. Both kittiwake and fulmar live most of their lives at sea frequenting the land only for the purpose of their breeding.

The tubenoses have the peculiar habit of defending themselves by shooting a penetrating oil rich in Vitamin A from their stomachs, through their beaks, at any intruder near their nests. Strangely enough, although I have watched fulmars, at a distance of a few feet on many occasions, whilst they have been engaged in their pre-nuptial displaying, and also whilst brooding their eggs I have never yet been spat at.

Purposely I eliminated from my study the terns, the tubenoses, and the skuas. I found it difficult enough to try to distinguish between a herring gull and the lesser black-back without having to try and pick out an arctic tern from a common tern. Most of the bigger gulls take quite a long time before they finally get their adult plumage, during this period it is not easy to differentiate between immature black-backs, herring gulls and sometimes even common gulls. Further, gulls sometimes interbreed. The herring gull and the lesser black-back have been known to do so on a number of occasions.

I knew, from my many bird books, that the herring gulls have flesh-coloured legs and yellow beaks whilst common gulls have yellowish-green legs and beaks and that the lesser black-back's legs are yellow. However, identification by their legs is not at all easy when watching gulls as so often they are observed whilst flying, when their legs are well tucked up behind their bellies, or whilst floating on the sea when their legs cannot be seen at all!

Beaks tell a lot. Herring gull's beaks are much more aggressive in appearance than those of the common gull.

The size of birds is a helpful indication of their species but size varies with age and so in itself can be confusing.

Habits are a help to identification. The black-backs and the herring gulls are greater frequenters of the sea than the common gulls and the black-headed gulls. The last two are frequently inland birds following the plough and in the case of the black-headed gulls nesting often far from the coast.

On one occasion I made for myself quite a reputation as a "bird-man" when I was on a botanical expedition in Rothiemurchus forest by the foothills of the Grampians. We were eating our picnic lunch on the shores of Loch-an-Eilan, across the water I saw a solitary black-headed gull perched on a rock. I thought his mate might be brooding her eggs in a nearby bed of rushes. I threw a small piece of biscuit as far as I could out on to the loch. The gull spotted my movement and flew over to investigate the morsel. In one lovely swoop he picked the bit from the surface. Within a few seconds another bird appeared. Gradually, by adding fresh pieces of my sandwiches and biscuits to the waters, I enticed the gulls, which now numbered eighteen, to within a few feet of where I sat on the banks of the loch. Although I did not succeed in actually getting the birds to take a piece from my hand, I had them swooping and circling all around my head! These birds were truly wild and not the sophisticated gulls of London and the Thames who live in continuous sight of humans.

Often I have despaired at ever being able to tell one gull from another but time, persistence, and practice, have made me gradually more expert. I found the problem of being able to tell one kind of gull from another a fascinating one, a sort of perpetual cross-word puzzle, in fact, but it has been great fun.

One day when I was with a party of expert ornithologists along the coast of Northumberland I saw a solitary bird floating in a cove below the ruins of Dunstanburgh Castle.

From its attitude I thought it was a black-headed gull. It was some distance from the shore and had its rump towards us. I asked a lady expert to confirm my identification.

"I think it is an Arctic tern" she said, as she examined the bird through a powerful telescope. Then the gull turned to show us its broadside. It *was* a black-headed gull.

Both sea gulls and land gulls are great scavengers. Refuse dumps in the cities and in the country are favourite places for their feeding. Many gulls are almost omnivorous. They are, also, in their feeding habits a strange contradiction. Herring gulls and black-headed gulls sometimes appear most fastidious in their feeding, washing as they do, in pools and the sea-water, their titbits before devouring them but both these species can be equally disgusting in their cannibalism. These bigger gulls have been observed to peck to death their own weakling young then to swallow them, regurgitate the remains, and feed the resultant mess to their surviving chicks. The kittiwake, of all the gulls, appears to have the nicest manners. So far they have not been observed to be cannibals and they do not scavenge to any extent. They gain their food from the living masses of the sea.

Many naturalists have made the gull their special study, names such as Goethe, Kirkman, Paludan, Tinbergen, Lockley and James Fisher come to one's mind.

Much has been written about these lovely birds. One of the most enthralling accounts of a naturalist's devotion to his subject is the story which James Fisher has recorded of the discovery of Ross's rosy-gull. The rosy-gull is a bird of the arctic. Its existence was not established until 1823 during W. E. Perry's second arctic expedition in search of a north-west passage. It was given the English name of Ross's rosy-gull after James Clark Ross who found it. Half a century later this bird was still only a legend. In 1879 when the American ship the *Jeanette*, on a voyage of exploration, became imprisoned in the ice near the New Siberian Islands large numbers of these gulls were seen over the pack-ice. R. L. Newcomb, the naturalist, shot eight of them. After the ship had foundered on 12–13 June 1881, not far from Henrietta Island, the expedition salved its collections to journey in the ship's boats across the Laptev Sea to the Siberian mainland. The leader of the expedition G. W. DeLong and many others died on the way but Newcomb kept three of his precious skins of Ross's rosy gulls under his shirt during this dreadful journey to bring his trophies back to civilisation.

This episode to my mind is a supreme example of the dedicated naturalist's devotion to his creed.

In spite of man's present, extensive knowledge of gulls there is still much to be learnt about them. To the ornithologist, and to those of us who are less expert, gulls have one great attraction; they are to be found throughout the world and its adjacent seas from the Arctic to the Antarctic—they seem to be almost everywhere.

14

WHOOPER SWANS

THE WILD whooper swan, the largest of our winter visitors, is a bird of great beauty. To see a flock of swans in flight is to me one of the loveliest sights in nature. Within a radius of ten miles of my home there are a number of lakes and ponds where whoopers regularly winter. Some of these stretches of water are artificial in that they have been created by man rather than by nature. Lakes like those at Catcleugh, near the Carter Bar, Bolam, Capheaton, Angerton and Linnheads are all man-made. There are others as well which are much favoured by the swans and these are the flooded pitfalls described elsewhere in this book. Pitfalls are particularly favoured by swans perhaps because most of them are shallow and the bottom feeding is good. Parties of whooper swans who spend any appreciable periods on these stretches of water often become reddish in colour; this I feel sure is due to the iron oxide in the soil which dyes their necks and breasts when the birds up-end to feed on the bottom of the ponds.

Sometimes you will find these great birds on the more placid stretches of our rivers. I once unexpectedly came upon a herd cruising in the water below the mill at Middleton on the upper reaches of the Wansbeck. Generally these birds are unmolested although undoubtedly along some of our coastal stretches the marauding gunman of our beaches blasts off his gun at the odd whooper or so. More than once I have come across the remains of dead birds amongst the rushy fringes of the pitfalls.

Numbers of whoopers arrive, in the autumn, to stay a short while and then they go elsewhere, others often attempt to stay the winter with us and they are certainly welcome visitors. Whoopers, who spend the winter here, seem more numerous than they were 25 years ago. Why this should be it is difficult

to understand for our winters are certainly no milder than they were a quarter of a century ago. If anything they seem to be colder and particularly the long icy blast which was the winter of 1962–63. Even during this exceptionally cold spell, when nearly every stretch of inland water was frozen solid, a number of whoopers were loyal to us. It was remarkable to see the way these great birds would try and keep a lake from freezing over completely. Gradually the ice would encroach from all sides to leave a little pool of open water now crowded with whooper swans and any other aquatic birds who could find space within its limits. When the ice eventually beat the birds by sealing their last remaining patch of water they seemed to take to any open stretches of running water rather than the sea. It was not easy to get about the country much during the zenith of the cold winter of 1962–63 but I did manage to get down to the coast on one or two occasions. The sea was not frozen but the sand between the tide lines was like concrete. I never saw any signs of the whoopers although they were in the habit of frequenting a number of pitfalls within a short distance of the seashore.

The whooper swans who visit us during the winter months are believed to nest in Iceland and David Bannerman, in his *The Birds of the British Isles*, has given some vivid descriptions of the nidification sites of these birds in the sub-polar regions. Occasional pairs of whoopers have made desultory attempts to nest in Scotland but of recent years there do not appear to be any authentic reports of the successful rearing of a brood of Scottish wild swans.

Whoopers, I believe, are great family birds and a pair will often keep their young with them all through the winter after their hatching. Quite often a family party, of four to six birds, arrives in Northumberland and will spend the winter here as a unit. I had the pleasure of observing one such family group all through the winter of 1962–63.

On the numerous pitfalls which dot the countryside, around the coal bearing areas of the county, there are occasional pairs of mute swans. The easiest way to distinguish the mute from the whooper swan is by their head carriages and the colour of their beaks. The mute curves its neck when standing or swimming whilst the whooper holds his head straight up. The whooper's beak is banana yellow whilst the mute's is orange. Once you get to know them it is quite easy to identify these birds both on the water and in flight. The whooper appears to be much more gregarious than the mute swan. The presence, however, of mute swans on a pitfall seems to attract whoopers to it. It is possible that the sight of a pair of permanent residents indicates to the foreign visitors that there is good feeding available. Once whoopers come down on water, frequented by mutes, they do not associate but keep in separate parties. The presence of the one species, however, does not drive off the other. I find it far more difficult to pick out a whooper swan from a Bewick. The neck carriage and beak colour of the Bewick are very much the same as the whooper's and size seems to be the only reliable distinguishing criterion, therefore, unless these birds are seen alongside of one another they can be confusing. Some people maintain, and they are probably quite right, that the Bewick is so much smaller than the whooper that identification is easy—I have not found it so although on occasions I am sure I have seen Bewicks but they are far scarcer than whoopers up in this part of the country. The cry of the whooper swan is one of the most thrilling sounds I know. To listen to a herd of whoopers coming over the hills with their haunting voices calling *whoop, whoop, whoop*, continuously, is a sound never to be forgotten. It is surprising how often one can be deceived by the call of the whooper for at a distance their chanting resembles, to a remarkable degree, the chorus of a pack of hounds in full cry after a fox. In hill country like that of the Cheviots I have been misled, on more than one occasion, thinking that I was listening to hounds babbling when in fact the cry was that of a flight of whooper swans.

★ 15 ★

WOODPIGEONS

THE FOUR RING doves burst from the locust tree as if the tree itself had exploded. With an astonishing burst of speed they fled out of sight around the bend in the narrow gorge through which I was walking. It was the first time I had ever seen a woodpigeon in Mallorca and somehow the sight was exciting. Although my first view of these birds was a very quick one I saw them again on two subsequent occasions, in the hinterland, behind Paguera, where I was staying in February. The extraordinary brilliance of the plumage of these pigeons was most striking. The clear bright sunlight of the Mediterranean day undoubtedly brought out their colours. The pale pink breasts, the white bars on the wings and the white clerical collars all stood out in remarkable clarity. Somehow, in Britain a woodpigeon is a dowdy bird in his grey dress but here in Mallorca these four ring doves were startlingly brilliant, far more so I thought than even the multi-coloured hoopoe. Perhaps this was because woodpigeons in the Balearic Islands seem to be much scarcer than hoopoes. I shall always cherish my first sight of *Columbus palumba* in Mallorca.

The woodpigeon, here in Britain, is a greatly detested bird. I have a garden and the appearance of my brussel-sprouts, after the pigeons have been at them, is, as if the locusts had arrived in the British Isles. Nevertheless, spring, without the voice of the dove with his *tak-two coos do—tak-two coos do*, would surely not be the same. Because woodpigeons are exceedingly destructive to agriculture they have, during recent years, received considerably publicity in the press. The farming interests want as many pigeons destroyed as possible. The use of dope in their feeding places is being tried. Traps, of various kinds, have been designed some of which are quite efficient. Organised shoots are arranged but still the woodpigeon survives. He appears to be an indestructible bird. His capacity for breeding through many months of the year and his widely scattered nesting habits have undoubtedly contributed to his survival.

Frankly, I would hate to see the same thing happen to the woodpigeon as has happened to the Passsenger pigeon in America. The last Passenger pigeon died in Cincinnati zoo in Ohio in 1914. It has therefore joined the dodo and the great auk as an extinct species. The Passenger pigeon was strikingly like our own woodpigeon, or ring dove as he is quite often called, to my eye the Passenger pigeon looked rather like what one might expect a cross to be between a woodpigeon and a turtle dove, if such a thing were possible.

The total extinction of the Passenger pigeon has been attributed to man's indiscriminate slaughter, although other reasons have also been put forward such as disease, disaster to thousands flying into the sea during migration, and the destruction by man, of their breeding habitats.

Some of the records of the slaughter of these birds are quite amazing. Audubon, the great ornithologist and bird artist, has left a remarkable account of the fearful butchery of these birds. For three days on end, he writes, the skies above the Ohio river were black with birds who were migrating in search of food. Every form of artillery was turned out to stem the hordes and still they came.

That the Passenger pigeon was a destructive bird there is no question. Their communal nesting habits, like the roosting habits of our own starlings, resulted in the wholesale destruction of woodlands. The weight of their numerous nests broke down the branches of the trees. Their droppings fouled the soil. Their presence in the oak and beech woods entirely stripped the trees of their acorns and beechmast. The Passenger pigeon was also a good bird to eat. This contributed to his eventual passing. The communal nesting habits of these doves may well have assisted in their eventual extinction for the squabs were considered a special delicacy. Wholescale attacks were organised when the breeding season was on, nets, traps and even cannons, shooting birdshot, were employed against the massed concentrations of these birds. Whether man himself was responsible for the eventual elimination of the Passenger pigeon will never be known but that he contributed his quota towards its extinction there can be little doubt.

At one time it was generally accepted that large numbers of woodpigeons were in the habit of migrating across the North Sea from the Scandinavian countries to spend the winter here with us in Britain. Today some doubt exists as to whether many birds from Norway and Sweden visit our shores.

Physically I can see no reason why woodpigeons should not travel considerable over-sea distances. Much smaller birds, with no better travelling equipment, frequently travel long distances over water.

The ringing experiments which have been carried out by ornithologists on woodpigeons have not yet provided any conclusive data about the pigeon's journeyings. The limited results obtained so far tend to show the woodpigeon as being rather a sedentary bird. He is also long-lived. I have a record of a woodpigeon, ringed locally, who was shot recently in the neighbourhood where he was marked, he was eight years old. A certain amount of ringing has been done on squabs in Scandinavia. One marking station at Stavanger in Norway reports no recoveries from Great Britain but rings have been returned to Stavanger from as far afield as Spain and France. This evidence certainly proves that woodpigeons are, at least, in some instances, migratory in their habits.

Having once accepted the belief that great numbers of woodpigeons were foreigners and not native-bred birds it is not easy to turn around and immediately accept the theory that when vast flocks appear in a particular neighbourhood they are mostly of British origin.

The results of limited ringing, carried out in the county of

Northumberland where during the winter considerable numbers of woodpigeons are always killed, show little movement. Of thirteen rings recovered from birds ringed within the county only one ring came back from over the sea and this was a ring recovered from a bird killed in Tipperary. Admittedly these small-scale ringing experiments do not necessarily prove that hordes of foreign-bred birds do not visit these islands *but* they may be taken as some indication that home-bred birds will stay put as long as they can get sufficient to eat.

In Northumberland there may have been two decided factors of recent years which may have resulted in an increase in the local population of woodpigeons.

A considerable area within the county has been afforested with conifers. These woodlands provide excellent nesting places for pigeons. We have no grey squirrels in Northumberland to take the pigeon's eggs and young.

During, and since, the 1939–45 war much land has been put under the plough so that there is a considerable acreage of cereal and green crops, excellent feeding for woodpigeons.

I believe myself that we have today in Northumberland far more native birds than ever before. Woodpigeons, like many other birds, flock to feed. Concentrations of pigeons observed in flight are usually travelling in search of food or, if seen in the late afternoon, are returning satiated to their roosting sites.

These concentrations can be confusing to the observer. On some days the sky appears to be full of birds and on others, for no apparent reason, few pigeons are seen. As this subject of the pigeon's migrations is as yet not-proven you still get the individual who says "I never did believe our birds were anything else but locally bred". Then there is the opposing school who is quite certain that at certain times of year Britain suffers a mass invasion of woodpigeons from overseas.

I was talking to one of the invasion believers the other day.

"I've seen them coming in over the sea in their flocks," he told me, "and I live near the links in full view of the North Sea, so I should know, if anyone does", he added.

One of these days we may learn something about the woodpigeon's travelling habits but at the present time, we, certainly, do not know a great deal.

* 16 *

RING-OUZELS

I saw the bird, during the first week in May, when I was walking along the Capel Mounth path which leads from Loch Muick in Aberdeenshire to Glen Doll in Angus. The altitude was over 2000 feet and low clouds covered the hills in mist. The mist, as it often will, had magnified the ring-ouzel until it looked as big as a jackdaw. The ring-ouzel was perched on a great, granite rock by the side of the path. He was bobbing up and down and flirting his wings just as if he were displaying before a female bird. I stopped to study his behaviour. It was not until I saw something—which looked like a huge boulder—move in the mist that I realised the bird was not engaged in a pre-nuptial display. For the boulder turned out to be a big, black stag with velvet nubs on his pate which were the beginning of his embryo horns. There were three stags, altogether, in the audience before which the ring-ouzel chattered and curtsied.

The stags were curious and it was not until one of them approached the ouzel too closely that the bird flew off chattering indignantly. I skirted the path for a while so as not to disturb the deer. As I came through the mist, five hundred feet lower down the path, I noticed numerous other pairs of ring-ouzels in the ravine of the Capel Burn. After the long, cold winter we had had, I felt sure that I had come across an incoming migration of these high-land thrushes; for the ring-ouzel is, in fact, a dark-coloured, white-throated thrush just as our native garden blackbird is a negroid variety of the thrush family.

The birds all seemed to be very busy flying here and there as if they were searching for nesting sites after their long journey from overseas. The last occasion on which I had seen a pair of these mountain-loving birds had been in a deep ravine below Puig Maya in Mallorca during the previous February. I wondered, for a moment, whether any of the birds I was now watching could have come from the Balearic Islands. Not a very great deal appears to be known, as yet, about the migratory routes and destinations of these attractive high-land blackbirds. Bird ringing recoveries have not been numerous in the case of the ring-ouzel possibly because it is this bird's habit to build its nest in somewhat inaccessible places. The majority of ring-ouzels seem to breed at heights of well over 1000 feet. Ring-ouzels, however, have been taken, whilst on migration, in traps and have been ringed. There is at least one record of a bird ringed in Dumfriess-shire which was eventually recovered near the Algerian-Moroccan frontier.

Dr. Eric Ennion of the Monk's House Bird Observatory, Seahouses, has made a special study of the ring-ouzels of the Cheviot Hills. He has ringed a number of nestlings during recent years but as yet no recoveries have been recorded.

The general trend of travel of ring-ouzels during the early spring months appears to be from the central Mediterranean areas to the Scandinavian countries and the British high-lands although it is believed that many ring-ouzels nest in the Pyrenees and the Swiss Alps. No ring-ouzel has, I understand, been observed south of the Sahara. According to Bannerman and Lodge the winter habitats of numerous ring-ouzels are the Tunisian Mountains, the Moroccan High Atlas and the Sahara Atlas. It is suggested that the abundance of juniper berries in these localities may be the reason for their temporary residence in these places.

During both winter and summer months—wherever this bird may find itself—it seems to prefer high ground and it also seems to choose to make its migratory flights over mountainous territory.

In Britain, during the spring and summer, ring-ouzels are

to be met with in such places as Wales, the Lake District, the Pennines and the Scottish Highlands.

The nest of the ring-ouzel is not unlike that of the garden blackbird and it is frequently built in crevices and cracks and sometimes in some sheltered place out on the moors. The cup of the nest is often formed of mud cemented together. It is a durable structure.

James Alder of Newcastle upon Tyne who has made a lifetime study of the dipper or water-ouzel once told me that he frequently came across the nests of ring-ouzels in close proximity to those of the dipper.

Ring-ouzels are both insectivores and vegetarians in turn and they seem to be able to change from one diet to the other without difficulty. In Scotland and Northumberland, where I have observed these birds, they appear to live largely on insects during the spring and early summer. I once watched a hen ring-ouzel feeding her young with leather-jackets, in the Henhole behind Cheviot, until the youngster was almost bloated with grubs. Later in the year berries become the birds' mainstay for rowan-berries, elder-berries, cranberries and blaeberries are all equally relished.

Whatever our garden blackbird does the mountain blackbird would seem to do it better. His flight is stronger, he climbs higher, his warning note is shriller and in defence of his territory he is bolder than his more common relative, only in his love-song does the ring-ouzel give best to the garden blackbird.

During the course of my researches into the habits and activities of the ring-ouzel I happened to read what the Reverend F. O. Morris had to say about *Turdus torquatus* in his entertaining series of books *A History of British Birds*. One sentence in the chapter on ring-ouzels reads "They are good to eat." A long list of places and dates where ring-ouzels have occurred in the British Isles is given and also a number of instances where these birds were evidently shot for identification purposes. A surprising number of clergymen appear among the shooters. All too often nowadays the old hunter-naturalists like St. John, Colquhoun and Speedy are vilified for their practice of shooting birds which are now rare in

Britain. If for some reason or another the ring-ouzel had decided to refrain from coming to our hospitable shores one wonders whether these churchmen of the nineteenth century might not have been blamed for its absence!

The Reverend F. O. Morris writes that the ring-ouzel is known variously as the rock-ouzel, the ring-thrush, the moor-blackbird and the mountain blackbird. George Bolam in his book *The Birds of Northumberland and the Eastern Borders* gives the local name of the ring-ouzel as the hill-blackbird.

Later in the day, during which I had witnessed the arrival in some number of these attractive birds on the slopes of Capel Mounth, I caught sight of a dipper, or water-ouzel, displaying on a rock in the middle of the Capel Burn. The water-ouzel—like the ring-ouzel—has a distinctive clerical collar but this would seem to be the only similarity between the two birds for they are, in fact, two entirely different species.

The water-ouzel, or dipper, as he is now more often referred to in this country is mainly a resident and not a partial migrant like the ring-ouzel. The water-ouzel is a short, stumpy bird not unlike a huge wren. Mainly aquatic in its habits the water-ouzel can run submerged along the bottom of a stream in search of food, or when disturbed. It is a fascinating sight to see a dipper perform its submarine activities as it dives, runs and swims in clear water.

The Latin names of these two birds are much more apt than our English ones. The ring-ouzel is known scientifically as *Turdus torquatus* which translated means the thrush wearing a necklace whilst the water-ouzel is described as *Cinclus cinclus* meaning a bird that waves its stern, an accurate description of this bird's antics. Habits these two species have in common are their diet—in spring in the case of the ring-ouzel—of insects and their liking for water. I have noticed, frequently, whilst out on the high moors, that the ring-ouzel appears, nearly always, to prefer glens and corries where there is constant running-water. The water-ouzel, as his name implies is, of course, essentially an aquatic bird.

The similarity of the names of these two entirely different kinds of birds is often confusing to the amateur naturalist. However, nowadays, the tendency is to drop the title water-ouzel in the case of the *Cinclus cinclus* and to concentrate more on his descriptive name of the dipper.

The ring-ouzel should, I think, continue to retain this name although he is, in fact, a dark-coloured thrush with a white necklace. Chambers's Twentieth Century Dictionary describes the word ouzel as meaning a kind of thrush so that, if we can rely upon this authority then the ring-ouzel has a perfect right to his name.

17

REDWINGS

MANY MEMBERS of the thrush family are great travellers. The ring-ouzel winters in the Atlas mountains in North Africa and nests in the spring in the high hills of Scotland. Redwings nest in northern Norway and then, having reared their broods, travel south for the winter. On one occasion, I am almost sure, I saw a number of redwings in the Balearic Islands. Both fieldfares and missel thrushes move about a lot and fieldfares, in particular, often keep in company with the redwings during their travelling periods. Blackbirds and song thrushes certainly shift their quarters at certain times of the year and, of recent years, parties of blackbirds have been observed in the spring travelling northwards.

The massed flights of such birds as the fieldfares and redwings, although not as spectacular as the fantastic, regimented aerial manoeuvres of a flock of thousands of starlings, are nevertheless interesting sights to the ornithologist. I once witnessed a rather unusual mass migration of redwings not far from the coast of Northumberland in the month of November. It was a day of low cloud which cleared towards evening when the temperature began to drop appreciably. I had gone to a plantation of larch and sitka spruce on the east of the A.1 road a mile and a half north of the market town of Morpeth. The time was just about an hour before dusk. As the sky cleared visibility became very good. Standing in the ride between a regimented square of spruce, with a strip of young larches in front of me, I could see a long way towards the North Sea. As my back was to the west the setting sun was be hind me. This clarified the view, in front of me, and also put me in the shade, as it were, to any birds flighting in from the east. The first birds to come in to roost were woodpigeons. They appeared as tiny specks in the sky to plummet into the tall tops of the conifers behind me. Seagulls, mostly in nice, neat V formations, now began to fly, in the opposite direction, towards the coast. Intermittent small packs of starlings then started to come inland passing over the fir trees but none of them perched in the plantation. Towards dusk large numbers of rooks appeared travelling high in irregular, wavering masses heading northwards to their various roosting places in the hardwood groves in the valley of the river Coquet. I heard the plaintive *si, si* of a pair of goldcrests and then I spotted the two birds as they darted here and there around a larch tree almost like a pair of flycatchers. The murmuring of the starlings as they undulated overhead en route for the extensive rhododendron plantations by Linden was the dominant sound in the still, winter evening.

Suddenly a party of eight redwings flew straight into the tips of the spruce trees behind me. They were followed, almost, at once, by a lot of ten birds. In a remarkably short space of time the whole sky to the east appeared full of small birds flying straight into the setting sun. The pink after-glow, left by the receding sun, exaggerated the natural rufous colouring of the incoming migrants and brightened their reddish flanks and wing-linings so that these appeared blood-red. The redwings now began to arrive in their hundreds packing the trees in front and behind me until the branches were laden with the weight of their many bodies. An incressant *seep, seep, seep* filled the air. The sound, rising above the coming wind, seemed to envelop everything. The noise made by the birds with the fluttering of their wings and the scrabbling of their claws as they clutched for some perching space amongst the trees pervaded the atmosphere. The vast concourse kept on coming. Every available perch in the woods behind and around me became occupied by these little northern thrushes. The visitors appeared to be quite oblivious of my presence there in the wood and even when I raised my stick to tap the bole of a spruce beside me the birds hardly lifted from the branches. They seemed to be dead weary from a long journey. The usual inhabitants of the wood were obviously not pleased with this invasion. One or two cock pheasants were audibly proclaiming their annoyance. Three jays kept flying up and down the rides calling in indignation. The woodpigeons had long ago departed to less populated haunts.

The sun had now set in a brilliant blaze of scarlet. Crimson edged clouds formed a barrier along the western horizon. When the pink afterglow had dwindled, to give way to the darkening, the incoming stream of birds began to lessen until finally a few, lone stragglers were all that remained of the visiting hordes.

But now came the short-eared owls, themselves possibly migrants too, who had followed the travelling redwings from over the North Sea. These big, broad-winged birds, with their harrier-like flight, weaved their ways amongst the tall tops of the spruce trees, killing when and where they willed. In the dim light I noticed a pair of hawks harrying the occasional redwings disturbed from their perches. Some of the little thrushes, evidently exhausted after their long journey, fell from the branches of the conifers on to the soft cushion of pine needles below. Foxes, weasels and stoats would soon be busy in the wood picking up the dead and the weaklings unable to maintain their perches during the night amongst the limbs of the sheltering trees. The plantation around me had become, in the space of an hour, a veritable larder for the predators both furred and feathered.

This invasion of redwings was a rare event to have witnessed. I have never seen exactly the same sort of thing happen before or since. This aerial landing with its vast concourse of redwings all chattering and rustling at the same time above my head, left an unforgettable impression on my mind.

The next morning the land was covered by a slight fall of snow. I went back to the wood and there on the tell-tale carpet of white were the tracks of foxes, hedgehogs and the occasional stoat. Several carrion crows flew off at my approach. They had evidently been feeding on the dead thrushes. Feathers there were in abundance with here and there tiny beads of scarlet blood on the whiteness of the snow. I found no bodies for most of such remains had already been taken by either predator or carrion bird. There was no sign of a living redwing in that wood for the mass had departed elsewhere on their long journeys southwards in search of food and warmth.

I wondered whether the killers, like the hawks and owls, were still with them on their great migration harassing their flanks as they flew in their restless wanderings.

18

STARLINGS

I HEARD, IN mid-November, a blackbird singing in the garden. The day was cold and bleak. A north-east wind brought with it flakes of snow which melted as they struck the crazy-paving stones beside the flower-beds. It was certainly not the sort of weather one associates with bird-song.

The blackbird sang again so that I had to go out into the garden to listen to this phenomenon. By the garden gate I looked up into the old laburnum tree to see a starling in full-throat perched on one of the topmost branches. Whether it stopped its song at the sight of me, or not, I do not know but the starling suddenly broke off its singing and began the characteristic chattering call of this species which is made by clashing the upper and lower mandibles of its beak one against the other. The rapidity with which this was done was so swift that my eye could scarcely trace the individual movement of the two parts of the bird's beak. Whilst chattering away the starling's beard bristled and the bird's throat feathers stuck out like the erectile prickles of a rolled-up hedgehog.

Starlings are known to be great mimics. The songs of the blackbird and the thrush are amongst the commonest in their repertoire but they will attempt to imitate the melodies of the warblers when these birds come to us in the spring. There are few bird-songs which the starling will not, on occasion, attempt. One of the finest items in their programme of mime is their most successful mimicry of the spring and autumn calls of that delightful wader the curlew.

On more than one occasion during this past year our local starlings have deceived me that the curlew had arrived, to set about their nesting, by a starling on the roof-gutters uttering the long-drawn, plaintive notes of *coor-lee, coor-lee, coor-lee*. The call, in fact, which has given its owner the name of curlew.

In some countries abroad, the starling's mimicking ability is commercialised because these birds are kept in cages like talking parrots for their remarkable vocal talent. It has been said that sometimes the starling's tongue is split so as to make the bird an even better vocalist but I rather doubt whether such a delicate, and possibly dangerous, operation is carried out now for the starling is a sufficiently expert mimic without any such cruel mutilation.

In the field of agriculture starlings have recently been very much in the news. Some farmers regard the starling as a pest others consider his presence in their field a benefit. As a grain-eater the starling can be harmful but again as a devourer of harmful insects he can be beneficial. As a tick-bird the starling stands high and it is a common sight in this country to see these birds perched on the backs of sheep and cattle busily engaged in ridding these domestic beasts of their insect guests.

Some scientists believe that starlings may well be carriers of foot-and-mouth disease but, so far, this accusation has never been proven. Why it is not possible to shoot starlings, on a farm which has been sequestrated after an onslaught of foot-and-mouth, and then examine these birds for signs of the virus I do not know but without doubt there is some very valid reason why this has not already been done—but so far I have failed to find the answer.

In town and cities, as well as in plantations and woodlands, starlings can become a pest when they elect to use such places for their mass-roostings. Bangs, bonfires, firecrackers, radar-waves, electrified wires, stuffed owls, and mechanical screeching devices, which imitate cat-calls, have all been tried in order to get rid of starlings from some of their favourite sleeping haunts but none of these methods, so far, has been of great success.

One of the most marvellous sights in nature is the massed-flight of starlings and these take place in their most spectacular form during the morning and evening movements from the birds' roosting sites to their feeding places and return.

How it is possible for vast congregations of birds to fly at high speed in densely packed formations without an occasional collision is almost beyond the comprehension of man. Looking up an old book on natural history the other day I learnt that a gathering of starlings used to be referred to as a murmuration of starlings, a more apt name it would be difficult to find for all the time starlings are in flight they appear to utter a constant muttering sound.

Starlings in this country today are seldom eaten but in certain continental countries they are considered a delicacy. During the 1939–45 war many people in this country ate starlings although in the majority of cases, I feel certain, that the consumer did not know the species of bird on his plate as starlings frequently masqueraded on the table as snipe, golden plover or woodcock. In a delicatessen shop in Church Street, Kensington I once saw a platter laden with starlings *en gelée* they were labelled sand-grouse! I do not doubt the birds prepared thus were perfectly edible. Far more unappetising birds than starlings could often be seen displayed for sale on the London poulterers' slabs for it was not unusual to see such sights as sea-gulls, moorhens and mergansers during this recent hungry period in our history.

Not long ago I happened to be crossing the North Sea, from Gothenburg in Sweden to Hull, in a cargo boat during the month of March. When we were half-way across the North Sea the steamer met a mixed migration of fieldfares, redwings, finches and starlings. During the night two starlings collided with a lighted porthole. The following morning a Swedish fellow-passenger brought me these two birds to examine. He was quite amazed at the beauty of the starlings' irridescent plumage.

"What kind are these lovely birds?" he asked me.

When I told him they were common starlings I think he hardly believed me and I can well understand this as few people unless they have actually handled a starling, in spring plumage, realise the glistening beauty of these birds' feathers.

The truth is that if the starling was a comparatively rare bird in this country, instead of an extremely common one—which he is—then because of his wonderful vocal talents and his remarkable plumage he would be very highly regarded both by the ornithologist and the lay naturalist. In fact, he would probably qualify with the waxwing and the hoopoe as something to write to the papers about.

As it is, no-one really bothers very much about starlings except when they decide to take over the outside of man's dwelling places and woodlands for their nesting places when man then proceeds to try and get rid of them—so far without very much success.

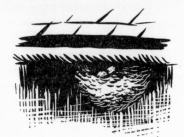

★ 19 ★

SWIFTS, SWALLOWS
AND MARTINS

AESOP, IN ONE of his fables, tells of the swallow who once gathered the other birds of the air together to advise them to dig up and devour the seeds of flax a farmer had recently sewn. For if you do not do so, said the swallow, men will contrive nets with the flax in which to entrap you. The birds took no notice of the swallow's advice and so many of them came to an untimely end; the swallow, however, being a cautious bird, betook herself to man that she might suspend her nest in safety under his rafters.

This apocryphal account of the swallow's acumen is not the reason for the swallow's preference for nesting in and about human habitations and like nearly all of Aesop's fables it credits his avian characters with a reasoning power they do not possess.

In this chapter I have grouped swifts, swallows and martins together. Ornithologically speaking this, of course, is incorrect for the swift is nearer the nightjars than he is to the hirundinidae but to the casual observer swallows, swifts and martins are all scimitar shaped birds, feeding on insects with a noticeably similar form of skimming flight. The skimming flight of these birds is deceptive in the speed sense. A great deal has been written on the subject of the speed of birds in flight. The truth is that the speed of a flying bird is not easy to estimate. Some of the figures given for the speed attained by swifts and swallows are obviously somewhat exaggerated.

The Reverend F. O. Morris says that the swift can attain a velocity of 180 m.p.h. and that the swallow travels at 90 m.p.h. In contradiction of these figures more recent writings have estimated the speed of the swift at 30 m.p.h. Further, there is a wide difference in acceleration between a bird swooping and one flying on a level course. Many attempts have been made to assess bird-speed with cars, aeroplanes and by timing their flight between two set points but we still do not know, with any degree of accuracy, how fast certain birds can fly. The flight pattern of the swifts, swallows and martins is particularly attractive and to the bird-lover there is no more pleasant sight than to watch these birds when they are on the hunt for the various insects they live on.

All these birds are summer visitors. Thousands of them come to the British islands annually to nest and breed. Over a period of years I have attempted to keep records of the arrival and departure of our local swifts, martins and swallows. From these notes a certain pattern emerges. The most pronounced of which is that the little sand martin seems to be the first-comer and the swift stays with us for a shorter period of time than any of the others. I live near the Scottish Border where the land of England is nearly at its narrowest, being approximately 70 miles from the north Sea to the Irish Channel. Through this funnel of land, in the spring and in the autumn, there is a great influx and efflux of migrating bird life.

The actual dates of arrival, noted by a single observer, are of little value but accumulated individual observations are useful as they can be co-ordinated to form a general picture of migratory periods.

In this part of the country the month of April undoubtedly sees the greatest incoming of all these species although the swift does not usually arrive in any numbers until May. August and September are the departure months but there are always early arrivals and stragglers. On one occasion in mid-October I saw on the top of Cheviot, nearly on the English-Scottish border line itself, a pair of swallows, at an altitude of over 2000 feet, apparently hawking for insects. However this is not exceptional as some observers have recorded the presence of swallows in this country as late as the month of December.

During the periods of migration the mortality amongst all these species of birds is known to be very considerable. Few ornithologists have not at some time or another picked up dead specimens. Nature seems to have provided for this high death-rate as most of these birds are multi-brooders and there are numerous authenticated cases of swallows and martins having hatched off three or more clutches of eggs in a season. The now popular habit of ringing birds has taught man a lot about them and particularly in the case of migratory birds, their nesting places and their winter destinations. Ringing also has shown that some birds can be very long-lived, in view of the hazards swallows have to continually contend with it is a little surprising therefore to hear of a ringed swallow who was aged thirteen years.

Of all these scimitar shaped birds the swift appears to have attracted unto himself the greatest variety of local names for he is sometimes referred to as the screamer, the screech and the squealer. In Northumberland the swift was occasionally called the swing-devil presumably because of this bird's habit of gliding in and out of the windows, and around the roofless walls, of old abbeys and churches, many of which are to be found along the Borders. Such places are still sought after today by swifts for their nesting sites.

The most attractive nickname for the swift is, perhaps, the Gaelic one of *Ghoblan Dubh* or black swallow.

Swifts have an almost uncanny weather-sense and there have been numerous records of these birds massing to escape the coming of electric storms; such an occurrence took place last year, along the north-east coast, where a number of competent bird-watchers recorded the mass-flight of swifts along the coast-line prior to a period of violent thunder storms.

Swifts, swallows and martins seek their food, on the wing, at various altitudes dependent on the presence of insect-life in the sky-level. When swallows fly high most country people have been brought up to believe that the weather will be fine and when these birds are flying low rain is likely. Thus we have the doggerel which runs:

> *"When the swallow flieth high,*
> *Then the weather's always dry:*
> *But when she lowly skims the plain,*
> *Ere the morrow there'll be rain."*

In the past the swift, like the swallow, was credited with all sorts of peculiar practices, they were thought to both mate and sleep whilst on the wing. There is some reason for the latter belief because swallows and swifts are both known to fly by night and during the pre-nesting period these birds perform their nuptial displays, high in the air, not infrequently appearing to touch one another. But I believe that coition usually takes place in or near their actual nesting sites.

Gilbert White, the celebrated eighteenth-century naturalist, made a special study of swifts, swallows and martins. In his day these birds were supposed to go in for a form of hibernation when they would immerse themselves in the mud at the bottom of lakes and ponds for the duration of the winter months. Migration was not as well understood as it is today and the tendency martins and swallows have of clustering on reed and bulrushes in the early months of autumn, prior to their departure abroad, may well have influenced the observer of these birds towards the belief that swallows and martins buried themselves in mud. Of recent years the naturalist, Dr. Maurice Burton, has shown that birds like the American poor-will—a distant relative of the swift—has been found to go into a form of partial hibernation accompanied by a slowed down heart-beat and a general lowering of body-temperature.

George Bolam, the famous Northumbrian ornithologist, has left records of cases where swallows and martins have arrived in this country, just prior to a late spring cold-spell, when the birds have resorted to old nests and other crevices, to lie dormant for several days, before emerging when the weather became warmer.

On one occasion when staying in the island of Mallorca in the Mediterranean, during the month of February, I awoke to the sound of strident squeaking as scores of sand martins flew around my balcony which faced the mountains of Mallorca. This mass-flight lasted for about a quarter of an hour during which period the birds appeared to be hawking for insects although I could see none of their prey although I had a pair of powerful Zeiss binoculars. The birds disappeared as quickly as they had come and I never saw a martin again that year during the whole of the three weeks I spent in the Balearic Islands. Whether I witnessed the beginning of the northern migration of these birds or a mass emergence from some sort of hibernation amongst the huge expanse of cracks and crevices which are to be found in the highlands of Mallorca I shall never know. Being somewhat of a sceptic, however, I am inclined to lean towards the belief that this was just a local gathering of these birds prior to their take-off for the mainland of Spain eighty miles north across the sea. Whether these birds were actually sand martins or crag martins I would not like to say not being a sufficiently expert ornithologist to be able to distinguish accurately between these two species.

The sand martin, a very common bird in Northumberland, and the Scottish Border counties has, in the past, been given the name of the Bitter Bank which is, in itself, self-explanatory as, in the majority of cases, these birds use holes in sand-banks and quarries to nest in.

The house-martin is not as common in my part of the north of England as is the sand-martin, however he comes to us every year and frequently in company with the swallows. Because of the house-martin's and swallow's preference for human habitations to nest in, they often come in conflict with the local house-sparrow population. Fights to the death over the nesting sites of these birds are not, by any means, unknown.

The swift, the swallow and the martins appear to be prone to forms of parasitic attention and, on occasion, individuals have succumbed as a result of an excess of such visitors—surely a case of the biter bit!

Although we are beginning to know a little about the habits and the various places of residence of all these attractive birds they are still mysterious creatures well-worthy of the naturalists' attention.

★ 20 ★

BLUE-TITS

I WAS READING a paper-back Western in bed. It was too early to get up. Through a gap in the velvet curtains I could see a glint of morning sunshine. The hero of my Western was a character by the name of Pal Joey, he was evidently a destructive though attractive type. The author described him as being as quick on the draw as a streak of sunlight.

As I lay absorbed in the doings of Pal Joey in his far-flung prairie lands I heard, suddenly, a considerable noise behind the drawn curtains. Looking over the the top of my book, to see what the commotion was about I saw a tiny, cobalt-blue head peep around the edge of the curtain into the room. The owner of the head apparently liked what it saw for it abandoned the space between the curtain and the open window to take up its perch on the wire of the central, pendant electric light shade. The blue-tit swung to and fro for a few seconds before deciding to try another site. The picture rail around the room seemed to afford the bird just what it was looking for. After a thorough examination of the premises the blue-tit decided to depart behind the curtains and out of the window.

Blue-tits have nested every spring in the niches of the old walls of our house They are fed regularly with scraps of bacon fat and other choice bits which we hang from the trees in little wire nets so that the sparrows do not get all the food. Of all the little birds the blue-tit is, perhaps, my favourite. They are such bold, brave, cheeky, little fellows. Their colours are superb. No man-created blue or yellow can quite match that of the blue-tit in full breeding plumage. They are truly exquisite beauties amongst our British garden birds, destructive little devils though they can be.

Next morning the blue-tit paid me another visit; it was then, I think, that I must have christened him Pal Joey in my sub-conscious mind, for ever after that I thought of him as Pal Joey or P.J. for short. He certainly did flash around my room like a streak of sunlight! Up till then he had shown no signs of his damage potential.

The wall-paper in my room is one of my most prized posses-sions. I brought it, in a series of awkward rolls, all the way from Paris in the immediate post 1939–45 war period when such things were practically unprocurable in this country. It is a delicate creamed coloured paper engraved with various minute figures of birds, beasts and hunters in a general *motif a la chasse*. Very soon Pal Joey began to appreciate my taste in wallpaper for, perched on the brass picture rail, he proceeded to peel my precious mural decoration in strips from off the walls. Catching him one morning, *in flagrento delecto*, picking away at the wall-paper I shooed him unceremoniously out of the room. He seemed indigant at the treatment I was giving him. He returned the moment my back was turned. I shooed him out again and shut the window.

That afternoon I left the car in the road outside the garden gate. When I went to put it in the garage Pal Joey had taken over. What there was inside this modern, all-metal, mass-produced vehicle to have tempted my blue-tit I just cannot imagine. Admittedly inside the dash-board locker there resides a paper bag of peppermint bullseyes, but how was Pal Joey to know this! I caught Pal Joey against the back window of the saloon and launched him into the air. He did not go far, he simply flew to the stone ledge above one of the dining room windows and sat there chattering with evident indignation.

Shortly after this episode Pal Joey transferred his attentions from my wall-paper to the lamp shades; these he used to pick at methodically all around the top and bottom rings until they finally began to disintegrate. Only once did I catch him at work on the lamp shades, though there was plenty of evidence of his destructive capacity in the shredded shades and the circle of paper chippings on the floor.

One evening on going up to my bedroom, at ten o'clock, I found Pal Joey roosting on the picture rail. I tried to catch him, quite unsuccessfully. I was not going to spend the night with Pal Joey in the room. I determined to get rid of him. No amount of urging him towards the fully opened windows was successful. He just did not want to face the dark cold outside. Finally I found an old landing-net in the gun room with which, in the past, I had taken many a fine slender troutling.

The hunt which ensued was quite something. Twice I had Pal Joey in my net but on both occasions he broke me, or more precisely he somehow managed to slither his quick, slender body through the fine meshes of my landing-net. After a quarter of an hour of ferocious hide and seek I was sweating profusely. Pal Joey was gasping almost audibly, his tiny beak agape. I felt a brute. Eventually I managed to get the net down over Pal Joey on the floor. I had him. I launched him out into the dark of the night. He did not like it at all as he tried to come back again but I shut the window on him. Next morning with the first glint of sunlight he had returned, quick as the first streak of sunlight!

This is the first year we have not had numbers of blue-tits about. Not a pair has nested in the walls or in the boxes we now provide for them. I wonder where they have all gone. The winter of 1962–63 was devastatingly long and severe. Many birds perished and I thought, or rather hoped, that the blue-tit would come through but like the wrens and the robins both of which are decidedly scarce this summer neither Pal Joey, nor any of his kind, have honoured our garden.

In some years blue-tits seem to be particularly numerous. Not so many years ago, it was in Pal Joey's time, blue-tits became a perfect menace in London by attacking milk bottles left by the milk roundsmen. Conjecture, as to what the birds were really after, raged through the press. Was it the wax tops or the layer of cream inside? Blue-tits love fat and so it looked as if the milk bottle bait might be either wax or cream. Suddenly the blue-tit invasion, if it was an invasion, ceased. One seldom hears of milk bottles being attacked these days. These "mass movements" of blue-tits seem to take place all over the country for whilst London had its blue-tit plague we had one too up here in the far north of England. I use the two words "mass movement" advisedly, instead of the one word "migration" because our British species of blue-tit, as opposed to the Continental variety—I can never tell them apart—don't seem to be great on migration. The milk bottle attacks were supposed to have been done by Britishers and not Continentals although some ornithologists did suggest an invasion of these islands by European blue-tits from over the Channel.

David Bannerman in *The Birds of the British Isles* states that blue-tits stood up well to the severe winter of 1946–47—perhaps 1962–63's winter was longer and harder. I think it really was. Anyhow, I am convinced it killed a lot of our local blue-tits.

Up here they have got some lovely local names for these birds. I like "ox-eye" but perhaps one of the best is "Biting Tom". The blue-tit got this label because it used to peck little boys fingers who dared to pry into its nest.

More general names are Tom-tit and blue titmouse. I only know of one bird of this species named Pal Joey and he was certainly a friendly soul and quick as sunlight.

★ 21 ★

THE GANNETS
OF
THE BASS ROCK

ON A DAY of glorious summer sunshine in the month of July I
set out from North Berwick harbour for the Bass Rock. North
Berwick, once a quiet fishing village where nothing happened,
is now a popular seaside resort with milk-bars, yacht club,
built-in swimming pool, donkeys on the beach and innumerable
gift shops. On most Sundays and Saturdays, in the summer,
this little fishing village is thronged with visitors from Edinburgh and the Border towns. It was warm in the harbour and
a smell of heated tar, engine oil, and the sea, rose to greet us as
we descended the steps of the landing stage to board the boat
which was to ferry us across the three miles of sea to the Bass
Rock. Outside the breakwater the sea's surface was dead calm.
It had an oily appearance which was strongly reminiscent of a
tropic sea. There was scarcely a breath of wind and the sky
above was a deep, cloudless blue. Flotsam, on the water's
surface, could be seen from a long distance away. Before we
reached the island we had observed guillemots, puffins, gannets, shags, herring gulls and a solitary razorbill. We stepped
ashore on the rock below the lighthouse, across the deck of a
fishing vessel which had accompanied us from North Berwick
for no one is allowed to land on the Bass unless from a registered
fishing boat.

Taking the concrete pathway which leads past the lighthouse
we climbed the steep slope to the tiny, derelict chapel said to
be the original hermitage occupied by St. Baldred in 756. The
present twisting cement stairs and pathway, flanked by iron
railings, passes, within a few feet of the rock's summit and then
over and down again to the great iron foghorn facing the Isle

of May which can be seen, on a clear day, well out in the Firth
of Forth. The heat haze on the day we visited the Bass Rock was
such that the island was like a blur of cloud on the indistinct
horizon.

I have heard it stated that on the Isle of Lundy in the Bristol
Channel where gannets used to breed that they departed owing
to the noise of Lundy's foghorn. The Bass Rock gannets seem
to like the boom of the giant iron trumpet for they nest in their
hundreds almost beneath its horn.

The Bass Rock has a romantic history for in the seventeenth
century it was used as a prison for political offenders and subsequently it became the last stronghold of the Jacobites in the
British Isles for four young adherents to the Stuart cause held
this little rocky island, for three long years, against all the
forces brought against them by the English king. These stub-
born men were finally brought to starvation but for their
courage they fortunately received honourable terms on their
surrender.

The Bass Rock rises to a height of 313 feet and it is about a
mile in circumference. On all sides, except for the landing
stage below the lighthouse, the cliffs of volcanic greenstone rise
sheer out of the water. Because of its scanty soil vegetation is
sparse on the island with the exception of the remarkable tree
mallow which flourishes on the Bass. This somewhat rare weed
is aptly named for, at a short distance, the clumps of mallow
look very like miniature pine trees.

Arriving near the peak of the island I decided to have my
packed lunch near the summit where there was a pile of loose
rocks the remains of some stone structure. All around this ruin
were the nests of herring gulls and a number of the parents
were engaged in feeding their young. The adults kept up a
persistent screaming as I ate my meal. To most people interested
in birds the Bass Rock is synonymous with the gannet. Below
and around the red-lead, painted, iron foghorn colonies of
these great goose-like birds had nested. The gannet, the only
member of the family *Sulidae*, is nearer to the pelican than the
goose. The name solan goose by which the gannet is also known
is therefore something of a misnomer. At times gannets fly
rather like geese over the sea's surface, low above the water, in

Indian file. They are white, or at least the adults are, and their
great wing span, which may surpass six feet, is in excess of
that of most wild geese. It was a fascinating sight up there on
the Rock's top to watch the gannets below flying to and fro
from their nests to the sea in search of food for their nestlings.
The great variation in the plumage of the adolescent birds was
very marked. Gannets lay one egg usually, on the Bass, towards
the end of April. The incubation period is believed to last just
over 40 days. Both parents participate in the building of their
nest, the incubation, and the management, of their solitary
young.

The pre-mating play of the adult gannets is well worth
watching and particularly the bill scissoring engaged in by
these big birds as they sit on their tails and rub beaks.

Young gannets at one time were an edible delicacy and even
now it is legitimate in the island of Sula Sgeir, off the north-
west coast of Scotland, to take these birds for commercial
purposes. The Bird Protection Act 1954 prohibited the taking
of gannets throughout the British Isles but The Wild Birds
(Gannets on Sula Sgeir) Order 1955 gave the men of Ness, in
the isle of Lewis, a reprieve so that gannets may be taken outside
the close season which finishes on August 31st. The young birds
are caught with poles with nooses on the end, killed, plucked,
gutted and then salted. I have never tasted gannet but I understand it is far from unappetising flesh. At one time there was a
considerable market in solan geese in some of the big cities in
Scotland and particularly Edinburgh.

The gannet's submerging plunge into the sea, in search of
food, is a spectacular sight and is one that I have never ceased
to revel in. The young gannets, once they are fledged, take to
the sea where they seem to do a lot of drifting. There appears
to be a strong migratory urge, inherent in these adolescents,
which takes them south. The adults are evidently inclined to be
more sedentary.

The heat of the mid-day sun, as it beat on the rock out of an
utterly cloudless sky, was terrific and the glare on the shadeless
island hurt one's eyes. The smooth, unruffled sea disclosed the
bird-life on it in remarkable clarity, puffins, guillemots, shags
and eider ducks were all showing on the North Sea's surface.

I noticed two grey seals but the Bass Rock is not greatly favoured by these amphibious mammals as there are no good hauling-out places such as there are on the Farne Islands some miles further south.

During the exploration of the island I was surprised to come upon numerous animal bones which at first I found it difficult to identify until I found the completely mummified and odour-less tail of a pig. It was intriguing to conjecture how this relic came to be deposited on the summit of the Bass Rock. I think I solved the mystery eventually for once back on the mainland and on the way home in the car we passed through an extensive pig farm. I am sure that the bones on the Bass Rock and the pig's tail were the pickings of the herring gulls who had carried these succulent morsels from the mainland to their nestlings on the Rock.

Having landed us at noon the boat came back for us at five o'clock, all of us several shades browner or redder, accord-ing to our individual pigmentation, than when we arrived, for it had been nearly impossible on this bare, piece of volcanic stone to avoid the hot rays of the brilliant summer sun.

⋆ 22 ⋆

BIRD HYBRIDS

UNDER BOTH confined and domestic conditions hybrids are not unusual. The mule is probably the best-known example. On the other hand, in wild-life inter-breeding between different varieties is an exceedingly rare event. The one exception being, perhaps, amongst the so-called game-birds.

The cage bird fancier will cross various strains with the object of achieving certain results such as improved voice, a variation of colour and so on. Different breeds of domestic and racing pigeons inter-marry freely but under natural conditions the ring dove, the rock dove and the turtle dove have never, within my knowledge, crossed their blood. Farmers through the centuries have done a great deal of inter-breeding with the object of obtaining improved milk and beef yields from their cattle, a greater wool clip from their sheep and a better bacon cut from their pigs, but in the wild, animals seldom if ever hybridise. Although, during my lifetime, I have had much experience of wild deer, I have never met with a cross of any of the resident, wild British deer, the red, the fallow, the roe, the sika and the muntjac. Under confined conditions, however, wild animals of different varieties have been known to mate. The lion and the tiger have intermingled and produced young but such freaks are extremely rare.

Hagenbeck, the famous international showman of the last century, was a greater experimenter in hybridisation. He tried to cross all sorts of wild animals but he did not achieve a great measure of success. He never succeeded in getting a fox and a dog to mate, although rather surprisingly there is a common belief in this country that such a union is not unusual.

Racial discrimination is a very strong feature under natural feral conditions. Amongst the smaller wild birds, for example, I have never known of pairing occurring amongst any of the thrush family although some of these birds, to the human eye, appear remarkably alike such as the fieldfare, the missel-thrush, the red-wing and the song-thrush. The blackbird and the ring-ouzel are both thrushes and are so alike that they can hardly be distinguished one from the other except for the fact that the ring-ouzel wears a white collar and lives at a much higher altitude, than does the garden blackbird, but I doubt if they have ever mated. With all the hundreds of varieties of the smaller birds we have in this country it sometimes surprises me that there is not some degree of inter-breeding and yet I have never come across a case of hybridism in the lesser, wild, avian world. Because game-birds sometimes cross, a certain amount of work has been done by the scientists on this subject and particularly in Germany and Scandinavia.

The capercaille, that giant grouse-bird almost the size of a turkey, has mated successfully with his lesser relative the blackgrouse. It happens that the black-cock is a particularly beany bird and so perhaps it is not altogether surprising to find that he has crossed with the hen grouse and the hen pheasant as well as domestic fowls and bantams. Rather strangely the grey hen, or female black grouse, is a rather shy, diffident bird, but she has been recorded as having succumbed to the strutting favours of the great cock capercaille and hatched fertile eggs of the union.

Very rarely the red grouse has been known to breed with both the black-grouse and the pheasant and specimens of such cross-breeds are in existence in museums and private collections.

Bantams have bred with both grouse and wild pheasants. I know of a brood of phantoms which has been hatched off this spring within a few miles of where I live. Pheasants occasionlly mate with domestic fowls, nearly every year cases of this sort are reported in the sporting press.

Both the partridge and the ptarmigan appear to be very exclusive in their matrimonial affairs. I have not heard of a case of either bird going beyond his own kind. The ptarmigan, however, has been suspected of having had extra-marital relations with other breeds of grouse, this is mainly I suspect because of the ptarmigan's wide variation in plumage. The ptarmigan's plumage changes from a mottled, black, grey and orange in the summer to snow white in the winter. Such wide variety, at certain times of the year, might well suggest a hybrid whereas, in fact, the ptarmigan, at least, in his domestic life would seem to be as pure as his winter plumage.

★ 23 ★

WELCOME VISITORS

NORTHUMBERLAND, where I live, lies on the narrow neck of England which dwindles, like the throat of a man, towards the massive headlands of Scotland. About seventy miles of land separates the Irish Channel from the North Sea; here Northumberland and its adjoining county Cumberland combine to keep these waters apart.

This causeway of solid earth, with the Pennine Chain running down its spine, provides a convenient bridge for the various migrant land birds who fly from the cold northlands to the warmer southern climes for their wintering. In the spring they return, by the same route, to their nesting grounds in Northern England, Scotland, Iceland and the Arctic regions.

In recent years the press and the local broadcasting stations have sometimes reported the appearance of unusual bird visitors to Northumberland. These may either be birds who have gone too far north in their spring migrations or alternatively some who have come too far south in their autumnal wanderings. These news items are published because, today, many people are interested in natural history and particularly in ornithology. What constitutes an unusual bird it is impossible to say for to some, who live in the south of England, birds like the nightjar and the turtle dove are no rarities but to us in Northumberland a sight of either of these species would be an exciting event. In over thirty years residence on the Borders I have never seen either a turtle dove or a nightjar although when I lived in Dorset both these were familiar birds to me. The nightingale is rarely recorded up here. One was reported on Holy Island in 1962 but in the south they are sweet-singing hardy annuals. The hawfinch, with the enchanting specific

125

name of *Coccothraustes coccothraustes*, is a rare bird to see in Northumberland and the annual sight-records are scanty, but in the fruit-growing areas of the south they can be a pest.

It is, I think, entirely natural that anyone interested in birds should always wish to view a rarity. Whether one is a specialist, interested in one particular species, or an observer concerned with bird behaviour, or just an ordinary bird-watcher, the sudden sight of some quite unusual bird can be extraordinarily thrilling and because of the sense of pleasure and excitement that such a sight can give, many of us, at times, see uncommon visitors that in reality are no rarities at all. This surely is because a view of a remarkable bird always gives one such immense satisfaction. Subconsciously, I suppose, we are always on the look-out for the rare. I think, perhaps, the bird who has bluffed me most has been the fieldfare. The colouring of this thrush can be astonishingly misleading and individuals appear to vary appreciably in their plumage. Light, in some way or another, can play all sorts of tricks with the fieldfare's feathers.

The sight of some birds, which are not unusual visitors, can also give one quite a thrill. I can never see snowbuntings, and I see them every spring and autumn during their migrations to and from their nesting grounds in the sub-arctic regions, without immense pleasure. Their flight, almost like a lot of little butterflies, is a pretty picture in itself.

Arctic skuas visit our shores every year and to the bird watcher they can provide an enthralling picture of piracy as they chase, harry and plunder the gulls of their rightful takings. Crossbills are on the increase up here, mainly because of the considerable expansion of our coniferous forests, but they are still quite something to have seen. The waxwing, probably because he is such a very handsome bird with his crest, his chestnut-pink plumage, his yellow tipped tail and his scarlet waxwing tips is usually seen every year but sometimes waxwings come in flocks whilst at other times they are solitary visitors. Waxwing years happen periodically and then you get winters when these birds are rarely seen. It is perhaps the irregularity of their appearance that makes a sight of them something to remember.

The great grey shrike is usually spotted by someone or

another each spring. Only twice have I seen this bird in Northumberland but both occasions were ones not to be forgotten.

The hooded, or Royston, crow is seldom a resident in this county but they are seen, as passage migrants, both in the spring and the autumn and sometimes in considerable numbers. Snowbuntings, skuas, waxwings, crossbills, shrikes and Royston crows are, to me, all birds the sight of which can give a thrill, mainly, I think, because they are out-of-the-ordinary. Such visitors I am sure are very welcome to all of us who are interested in birds. Obviously no single watcher can hope to see even a fraction of the real rarities which may visit his locality but it is nonetheless enthralling to hear, and if possible, check such local sight observations. This I have endeavoured to do ever since I became interested in birds. I have a number of little, red notebooks, now, which provide quite interesting reading. The checking of the authenticity of reports and observations, with co-operative field naturalists, can be a pleasure almost as great as bird watching itself; after all you are talking with people who are interested in the same things that you are interested in.

Sir John Craster of Craster, who is an ornithologist of considerable standing, once told me he saw a honey buzzard hunting a bare, bleak side road in northern Northumberland. We have no wild honey in the county and what attracted this bird to come here it is difficult to say. Since this sight observation there have been other records of honey buzzards within the county. Whilst on the subject of buzzards it is rather surprising, perhaps, that the common buzzard is quite a rare bird in Northumberland. I have only seen two, one on the top of Cheviot and another at Meldon near Morpeth. This scarcity of buzzards is somewhat mystifying because these birds are not unusual over the county border in Cumberland.

The roller, a bird of lovely colouring, a gradation of Oxford and Cambridge blues, has been seen in the colliery district, near Arcot Hall, within twelve miles of Newcastle upon Tyne. The observer, an entirely reliable person, was, as it happened, already familiar with rollers abroad.

One would scarcely expect to see a golden oriole so far north as Northumberland and yet one of these birds, a cock, was watched by two experienced ornithologists during the spring of 1952.

Another visitor who comes here occasionally from the far south is the hoopoe. One of the first recorded came and stayed for a few days on the Farne Islands. This was obviously a somewhat sensational appearance and there is a most interesting report of the hoopoe's coming, compiled by the late T. Russell Goddard, one time curator of the Hancock Museum, in the Ornithological Report of the Farne Islands of 1947. Since then hoopoes have been seen by a number of reliable watchers nearly every year.

Quails are uncommon in the county but usually the odd pair tries to nest. Whether these birds have of recent years ever succeeded in breeding here is quite unknown. I flushed a quail in a field of roots one September day at Hebron just north of the town of Morpeth on the A.1 road.

Corncrakes were not, in the past, rare birds in Northumberland but they are scarce today. This may be due to a change in our agricultural practices for the corncrakes like reeds and plenty of rough grass. Now and then, however, a crake puts in an appearance. Two rather strange records of this bird have come to hand within the past few years. A lorry driver, on his way southwards from Berwick-on-Tweed, heard a bump on his windscreen whilst driving in the dark. On unloading his cargo of sacked potatoes, after arrival at his destination in Newcastle upon Tyne, he found a dead corncrake amongst the bags! Another corncrake was discovered inside a public convenience at South Shields—one cannot but conjecture how on earth the poor bird ever got there or why it should select such an entirely unsavoury place in which to hide.

An avian visitor from very far away was an American dowitcher—a snipe-like bird—who spent some time near Killingworth on the north-eastern outskirts of the city of Newcastle last winter. Migration across the English Channel and the near landlocked Mediterranean is one thing but for a marshland bird to cross the Atlantic is certainly a remarkable feat of endurance.

Perhaps, no more wonderful, however, than the regular

crossing of the tumultuous North Sea by such tiny aviators as goldcrests. These miniatures' sea-voyagings, from Scandinavia to the British Isles, have never ceased to amaze me. Of recent years avocets have been noted on the coastal mudflats of north Durham and a crane was seen regularly last winter in this area but undoubtedly the most sensational recent record of a real rare bird is that of a Ross's Rosy gull picked up dead but still warm at Holywell Ponds near the coal town of Bedlington. This incident I have recorded elsewhere in this book, in my chapter on gulls.

⋆ 24 ⋆

AVIAN AIRLIFTS

It was the circling of the seagulls which first drew my attention to the bird. There must have been twenty or thirty gulls swooping and diving at him with their raucous calls.

The bird being mobbed was big and his wing beat was slow as he came on flying a few feet above the turbulent surface of the grey North Sea. It was cold with a biting wind out of the north-east. Cloud wrack hung like a wet blanket over the seascape. I watched the bird through my binoculars while he made his way steadily shorewards. When he reached the tide-line the gulls gave up their pursuit, perhaps they had come to the conclusion that their intended victim had nothing to disgorge.

Through my field glasses I could see the bird was an owl. I guessed he would probably be a short-eared owl as numbers of these birds visit us from across the North Sea especially during the winter months. Once he was over the brief beach the short-eared owl began to climb towards the cliff on which I stood. The top of the cliff was covered in coarse grass and dead bracken, here and there a storm-beaten elder bush sprouted from the barren soil.

The owl jinked when he saw me but he only flew a matter of some ten yards before he dumped himself down into a bunch of brown, frosted bracken. Then almost instantaneously with the landing of the owl a surprising thing happened for two tiny birds sprang out of the bracken bush. Before I could get my glasses on to them to identify them they had flown into one of the thick elder bushes. They only stayed there a minute or two before they were away again. I am almost certain that they

ere a pair of gold crests, but my ability to identify little birds,
t a glance, is certainly far from perfect.

I went back to my owl who let me approach to within a few
:et of where he sat amongst the bracken, when he finally saw
ae he took off in his slow lumbering flight towards the fir-
/oods, inland, by Cresswell. He was a short-eared owl, all
ight. I began to wonder whether I had just witnessed an ex-
mple of an assisted air passage across the North Sea. I cer-
ainly had not seen the gold crests on board the short-eared
wl but, at the same time, I'd witnessed something very much
ke a dis-embarkment!

That certain birds do carry their young in flight there is now
10 further doubt. The woodcock in this country is one illustra-
ion of a bird's ability to act as a carrier. The snipe has also
leen observed doing the same thing.

Very early one morning in the Scottish county of Moray
vhen I was out watching roedeer in the fir woods near the
nouth of the river Findhorn I witnessed a woodcock carrying
ler babies.

I was standing quite still in a sandy ride, which ran through
he woods, watching a fine roebuck thrashing a young conifer.
iuddenly out of the corner of my right eye I noticed the move-
nent of some creature in the fringe of heather which bordered
he path.

An adult woodcock rose from the heather and in slow
hythmic flight beat down the ride in front of me. Below her
lelly there was a pronounced bulge and her legs hung down as
f she had something tucked between her thighs.

I stood quite still to see what would happen. The 'cock
lew out of my sight over the tops of the fir trees but she was
lack again within a few minutes. She dropped by the clump
lf heather from which she had sprung. This time I saw her
:quat and she air-lifted another downling woodcock within a
/ard or so of where I stood. This sort of air transportation, of
:ourse, is quite a different thing to a short-eared owl carrying a
:ouple of gold crests across a great expanse of stormy sea.

Not long ago in a Scottish newspaper I read a remarkable
iccount of a wild mallard duck's ability to carry her whole
brood. The two witnesses of this event stated having seen a

mallard alight in a garden at Conon in Ross-shire with ɪ
less than *nine* diminutive ducklings on her back! The malla
is reported to have left her young to be cared for by the owne
of the garden as the matron mallard departed and nev
returned to her brood, perhaps she was exhausted by h
extraordinary domestic duties.

Ducks, of course, do occasionally nest in trees and some
these nests are placed quite high up. The reason, one mig'
guess, is to keep the eggs and the young out of the reach
foxes, coots, rats and other ground-predators. Much specul
tion has taken place as to how the ducklings—when they a
hatched out—reach the ground. No one I know has ev
witnessed the actual event although ducklings successful
brought off at altitude have subsequently reached *terra firm*
in fine fettle. My answer to this somewhat abstruse ornith
logical problem is that little ducks are somewhat like litt
rubber balls, they can take an awful lot of bouncing.

Colonel R. Meinertzhagen, in his recent, most absorbin
book on birds called *Pirates & Predators*, has devoted a coup
of pages to bird transportation.

The Colonel records a number of instances when shor
eared owls and gold crests have been found dead together b
the side of lighthouses after having struck the light of th
lantern. All these birds were most certainly killed during migr
tory flights.

Colonel Meinertzhagen also mentions the report in *Time &
Tide* of 9th December 1939, by David Haig Thomas, of th
shooting of a short-eared owl, after its arrival from over th
North Sea, when a gold crest was found to be clinging to th
feathers of the greater bird. I suppose the short-eared owl wa
shot as possibly even in 1939 these fascinating birds wer
considered vermin-to-be-destroyed.

Before I leave Meinertzhagen I think one of his most con
vincing stories of avian airlifts should be mentioned. This dea
with the incident which occurred during the last war when th
British navy were doing much convoy work to Russia in 194
and 1944. A naval officer on board one of our convoys fired at ɪ
flock of swans as they passed over his craft with his shot-gun
Anything can happen in war time. The italics are mine. The repor

f the gun disturbed quite a lot of small black and white birds
vhich had evidently been travelling in the swan's plumage.
'hey came fluttering out and were last seen following the swans
nd trying to remount but failed to do so owing to the faster
peed of the swans.

One reads these days, not infrequently, of passenger air-
raft being buzzed by fighters, or sometimes shot at, when over
resumably controversial territory but this is the first time I
ave ever heard of whooper swans with snowbuntings on board
eing subjected to shot-gun fire—not that I don't believe it.

There is a very old legend which relates that when the
olden eagle boasted to all the birds of the earth that he was
he greatest of them all and to prove it he would fly higher
han any other, a wren hearing this boast stowed away amongst
he great bird's downy underparts. When the eagle reached his
eiling and could climb no further the wren launched herself
nto the sky and fluttered up a few feet further and so gained
he fabulous title of greatness.

This is the first instance of an avian airlift I have knowledge
f.

★ 25 ★

TWO RARE NESTS
IN ONE DAY

I HAD PLANNED my walk the night before. I would leave th
car at Coylum Bridge on the north-east fringe of the Cair
Gorms Nature Reserve where the Lairig Path to Braema
begins its route through the ancient pine forest of Rothie
murchus.

When I drove my car up to the gates of Drumintoul Lodg
—where there is a convenient parking place—I noticed a tin
bird fluttering in a tall conifer by the drive gates. I was abl
to identify it at once as a gold crest—the smallest of all Britis
birds—smaller, in fact, than the wren by a quarter of an inch
For many years, I must admit that I believed that the tin
brown wren was the smallest of all our birds.

The gold-crest is a favourite of mine and I have never cease
to wonder at this little bird's ability to cross the North Sea i
all its winter roughness to visit these shores when on its autum
nal migrations. Most of these visiting gold-crests are said t
be of the Continental variety whereas it is the British specie
which normally nests in Britain; however, both birds are s
alike in size, colour, shape and habits that only the specialist
can possibly tell them apart. In writing of this attractive bird
the Reverend F. O. Morris, in his *History of British Birds*, say
that, "They are hardy and robust though of such tender make.'
How very right he was.

The gold-crest I was watching disappeared as suddenly as i
had shown itself. Through my binoculars I searched the conife
and all the nearby surrounding trees for a further sight of th
tiny creature. Suddenly I saw the gold-crest pop out from
under a branch some 12 feet above ground level. It was then
I found the nest which was a masterpiece of ornithilogica

134

architecture. Shaped like a large Easter-egg it was constructed of moss almost the exact colour of the conifer-needles. It was one of the most remarkable and craftily concealed bird's nests I had ever seen. I did not try to handle the nest or peer inside it. The sight of the nest itself was quite sufficient reward for me.

When I first entered the forest of Rothiemurchus I walked along the path, passed the Batchelor's Cottage and Whitewell until I came to the iron bridge which was once called the red bridge, but has now been painted grey. There were plenty of birds to see all the way from curlews through missel-thrushes to the tiny blue-tits. After crossing the Beinnhe burn by the iron bridge I went on until I reached a point where the Lairig path bifurcates. One route goes to the Wells of Dee, another to Loch Morlich, and the third to the Glenmore-Coylum motor road via the Mineral Wells; I took the last-named path.

At mid-day I stopped when I saw a parcel of red deer hinds and last year's calves feeding quietly in a glade in the pine woods. Being down wind of the deer I was able to watch them unnoticed from my selected seat at the foot of an old Scots fir. I had just finished unwrapping my sandwiches when a small bird flickered in the branches above. The crested tit was remarkably tame. I felt somehow that this particular specimen must have fed off cheese sandwiches before. Within two minutes of showing itself the tit flew off to a rotted pine stump. At the base of the stump was a hole, within the hole was the nest of the crested tit.

The crested tit, for a number of reasons, is another of my favourites. The bird is so essentially Scottish—more so, in fact, than even Scotland's accepted national bird the golden eagle, for the Scottish crested tit is a sub-species all on its own, and it is confined to a particularly ancient part of Scotland, namely, the old forest of Rothiemurchus, the Braes of Abernethy, Glenmore, and certain parts of the Spey valley. Further, the crested tit, as its name implies, wears a cocky crest not unlike a Glengarry bonnet—a Scottish headgear if ever there was one.

To find a gold-crest's nest and a crested tit's nest both on the same day and so entirely unexpectedly, was indeed a rare event. It was also something which, I am quite sure, will never happen to me again.

Not once during this memorable day was I tempted, in any way, to pry into either of these two rather rare nests for I am not the poking type. Another thing, I do not like the feel of a young unfledged bird. They are rather horrifying to me. Their nakedness and blind helplessness very nearly revolts me and then when they grow older and their feathers begin to appear in their blue quill sheaths, and their gaping, yellow rimmed beaks start to cheep they become even more sinister. This applies, in my case, only to those birds where the chick comes finally all-naked from the egg. Other species, like young pheasants, partridges, ducklings, curlews and ringed plovers don't worry me at all. In fact I find them most attractive tiny bundles of fluff. Not that I would ever go out of my way to handle a wild chick except to rescue it; this I once did to a tiny ringed plover on Cresswell beach. The mother plover had been put on the wing by a dog and was bravely doing the broken wing act to draw the brute away from her young. I saw one of the little ones run into a black viscous patch of mud. I picked up the chick who seemed to appreciate the warmth of my hand. I cleaned the bird as best I could and when the dog had disappeared and the mother plover had returned I put the little one down. The baby bird seemed none the worse of its adventure.

This aversion I suffer from for fledgling birds can be traced, I think, to a number of incidents I was subjected to when I was very young. Japanese boys, with whom I played near Yokohama, had a nasty habit of trying to stuff fledgling sparrows down my neck. My terror encouraged them, I am sure, to keep on with these acts of thoughtless cruelty until they were caught one day *in flagrente delecto* by my uncle who was an ardent bird lover.

Later, at my prep school in England, a particularly loathesome type delighted in trying the same trick on me only this time he used young swallows. It does not need a psychiatrist to tell me why I shudder at the too close proximity of a fledgling bird. Any bird's nest is quite safe from my inquisitive fingers or my prying gaze—that is until the season for nidification is well past.

★ 26 ★

BIRD'S NESTING
IN MID-WINTER

WHOEVER HEARD of such a ridiculous pastime as bird's nesting in mid-winter one might well ask. Strangely enough, however, it can be a most enthralling experience. You will not find any eggs, of course, but then I am not an egg-collector. Eggs of wild birds have fortunately never had any attraction for me. I collect other things and have got some quite nice stamps, three cabinets full of mediocre glass paperweights and one of the best collections of roedeer heads in Britain. I have the acquisitive streak in my make-up, alright, but it does not extend to birds' eggs. Frankly I hate to interfere with most birds domestic affairs. It seems almost indecent to me to pry into nests during the incubation period of their contents.

When I was young bird's-nesting was a very popular pastime both with boys as well as grown-up men. This pursuit to my mind was an almost entirely predatory practice. The attraction was not the architecture of the nests themselves but rather the eggs within them.

In some cases the collecting of birds' eggs made individuals into near-frenzied maniacs. Not that egg-collecting has yet ceased as is well illustrated by the recent act of sheer vandalism, on the part of an alleged collector, which resulted in the osprey's nest being robbed by Loch Garten in Inverness-shire. I have mentioned this incident elsewhere in this book.

The taking of wild birds' eggs for profit still goes on although much of it is now an underground affair. A senior officer in our local police force told me, recently, that he had had a visit from an inspector, in a different part of the country, who had a line, as they say, on a particularly large collection of eggs in the far north of England. The owner of this collection was suspected of supplying an unknown dealer with eggs in the south of England.

Careful inquiry of the suspect resulted in the discovery of the dealer in the south. Eventually other contacts were disclosed one in South Wales and still another in the Lake District. This "ring" was eventually tracked down and the activities of the individuals participating were drastically curtailed.

There is no doubt that today a number of events have conspired to change the mentality of the egg collector. The Protection of Birds Act of 1954, and its subsequent amendments, have made illegal the taking of the eggs of a large variety of birds. Severe fines and penalties may now result if anyone is caught robbing the nests of protected birds. Public opinion, too, has changed largely as a consequence of the attitude of the majority of the press of this country towards this practice. The education of children, in matters concerned with natural history, has helped toward the conservsation of our bird-life rather than its destruction, and egg-collecting can certainly be classified as a destructive employment.

To those of us who are attracted by the ways of the wild there is ample scope still for bird's nesting but in quite a different form from that in which this has been largely conducted in the past. This may sound a somewhat surprising statement to make but, in mid-winter, the exploration and discovery of birds' nests can be a most interesting and engaging employment. The construction and architecture of the nests of various different birds is a study in itself.

Not far from the house, in which I now live in the country, there is a narrow cart-track, bordered on both sides by untrimmed, straggling hedgerows. When the frosts and winds of late autumn have stripped these hedges of their foliage a remarkable series of birds' nests are exposed to view. Within a a distance of some 400 yards I have discovered seventeen nests. In spite of the fierceness of our winter weather many of these nests are in excellent order. Their construction and the materials of which they are made provide a fascinating subject for investigation.

The largest nest, by far, in this corridor of avian habitations, is that of a magpie. Alongside the nests of the other hedgerow dwellers it is a huge affair. This big, domed structure, made of interwoven twigs and branches, and lined with sheeps' wool and mud, is a permanent home resorted to every year by magpies and I imagine the same pair come back every spring to nest in their old home. At the far end of the lane is a tall tree, in the hedgerow, where a pair of carrion crows have built their strong nesting quarters. This too is sometimes used, again and again, in succeeding years by the same species. In between the big nests of these predatory crows there is a series of lesser nests made by such various birds as blackbirds, thrushes, wrens, chaffinches and starlings.

The nests of the blackbirds and thrushes are remarkably alike being mainly constructed of coarse grass and lined with caked mud. As both these birds are of the family *turdidae* it is, perhaps, natural that their nidification habits should have a marked similarity. Starlings are known to be extremely catholic in the selection of their nesting sites, holes in all sorts of places are often used but starlings will also appropriate an abandoned nest and with, perhaps, some fresh straw and hay, plus a few feathers and a little wool, bring forth a clutch in someone else's abandoned home.

The cup-shaped nest of a chaffinch, woven of moss and wool, was apparently a durable structure as was that of a yellow-hammer situated low down near the bank amongst a clump of frost-bitten bramble. Yellowhammers, I am glad to say, are still very numerous in this part of the country. Roadside spraying with potent chemicals has not yet defiled the verges of the cart track. It is doubtful whether the County Council even knows of the existence of this delightful lane.

There was, at least, one blue-tit's nest in that hedgerow. It was located in a hole in an old hedge-post. Fine grass, moss, bullocks' hair, sheeps' wool and feathers had all gone into its comfort. A wren had selected a site for its nest in a rotten stump. It was a most attractive affair made of dried leaves, cow hair and dry green moss. The dunnock, or hedge sparrow, was naturally an inhabitant of the lane. The dunnock's nest looked smaller but not altogether unlike a miniature blackbird's nest as it was round and made of fine grasses but instead of a cement-like floor it was feathered within.

Half-way along the lane, high up in a blackthorn bush, a wood pigeon had made a flimsy platform of a few twigs upon which she had presumably raised her squab or squabs.

The reason for the popularity of this particular stretch of cart-track, as a desirable nesting site for so many different kinds of birds, was not difficult to understand for the place was generally quiet and few vehicles, or people, frequented the place. The leaf in spring and summer is luxuriant affording the maximum cover and shelter for birds; it seems to have all the essential amenities. Within easy flying distance there are convenient fields of roots with their attendant caterpillars, butterflies and multitudes of insects. There are also extensive pastures where sheep and cattle graze, acting as hosts to myriads of flies and to provide as well hair and wool for the use of the many nest-builders. My winter hedgerow is in very truth a most desirable communal nesting site.

★ 27 ★

PITFALLS

On some bye-roads, in the colliery districts of the two counties of Durham and Northumberland, the motorist will occasionally come across notices which warn the driver of perils ahead. These read:

Beware Road liable to Subsidence

These cautions do not mean that whilst driving along the highway the surface will suddenly collapse to swallow you and your vehicle. The purpose of these notices is to slow down fast-moving traffic because ahead some gradual subsidence has occurred, or is likely to happen, on the road's surface. Road subsidence of this sort is caused by underground mining, for miles and miles of land, in and around the many coal-mining areas, have been tunnelled under, over the years, during the process of coal extraction. This labyrinth of deep-down shafts has caused the earth's surface to sink in many unexpected places. The roads themselves are not, by any means, the only spots to be so affected and pitfalls can happen in all sorts of places. I have watched, over a period of time, the appearance of a number of these sinkings. You never see the earth actually move for the process of the formation of these landfalls is usually a slow, gradual one.

When pitfalls occur on farmland one of the first things that happens is a natural collapse of any existing land-drainage system. The declivity when it becomes sufficiently deep then attracts moisture. Rains begin to fill the fall and before very long a shallow lake appears. Sometimes, for years in succession these shallow meres dry out, during the summer months, but over a period of time many of them become permanent pools of water. Once a pitfall starts, water-loving plants soon appear

and in a comparatively short time these ponds are surrounded
with aquatic vegetation. Common rush, reed mace, yellow flag
iris, marsh marigold, and buttercup, all commence to sprout
around the pools' fringes. It is probable that a lot, of the original
seeds of this form of vegetation, are brought on the feet of
birds for these spots are obviously places much favoured by a
considerable variety of birds. Starlings, rooks, jackdaws and
crows first find these damp spots good feeding areas but once
they become flooded the aquatic birds arrive and many of them
eventually take up a permanent resident on these ponds.
Migrant birds and other visitors also act as hosts to the spawn
of frogs and fishes so that the waters soon begin to teem with
life.

Not infrequently, the first aquatic avian residents are a pair
of moorhen, belligerent birds who are quite capable of trying
to see off other potential residents but they seldom succeed.
Gulls make a considerable use of pitfalls as they provide
excellent resting places when the weather at sea is stormy.
Black-headed gulls although they use pitfalls, do not regularly
nest in their vicinity simply because so many of these places
are located in fairly densely populated areas and black-headed
eggs are both delicious and, in any quantity, fetch good prices
in the market. Where a pitfall is on strictly protected, private
land, however, you will find all sorts of interesting birds nesting
in their neighbourhood. There is a fine pitfall near Seaton
Burn, within sight of the A.1 road from Newcastle upon Tyne
to Edinburgh, where snipe, mallard, coots and moorhens nest
in complete security for the land, on which it has occurred, is
well-keepered. Because a great many of these accidental lakes
are situated on grasslands the bottom, once flooded, becomes
attractive to the underwater feeding birds like the various
ducks, geese and swans and some of them, such as the big falls,
near Cresswell Bay on the Northumbrian coast, have become
permanent winter quarters for great birds like the wild whooper
swans. A well established pitfall pond can prove a most interesting place for the bird lover. I have spent many hours, at a
number of these places with my binoculars. Pitfall observation
is a favourite recreation of mine, during the weekends, in the
early spring and early winter, for at these seasons of the year

the places are much frequented by birds. The resident population is then also often greatly enlarged by visitors and passing
migrants.

To list the birds seen on these ponds would merely be a
tedious catalogue but it is no unusual thing to see such species
as whooper swans, teal, mallard, shoveller, shelduck, tufted
duck, wigeon, coots, moorhens, little grebes, and almost certainly a snipe and a redshank on the bank.

Many of these artificial lakes are within close distance of
convenient side roads where it is possible, in inclement weather,
to do some exciting bird-watching from a saloon car parked,
off the road, on the grass verge. This is a lazy form of ornithology but an exceedingly pleasant one, none the less, on a
cold winter day with the wind in the north-east which brings
with it snow and pellets of ice. The birds seek the seclusion of
these sheltered, land-encircled waters and you seek them, as it
were.

On one occasion watching from the car I saw a considerable
gathering of birds on the pitfall by Cresswell. With the aid of
my most excellent *Field Guide to the Birds of Britain and Europe*
I was able to identify the lot, but one bird I had never seen
before and it was undoubtedly to me an exciting view for here,
swimming in the middle of the pond, was a solitary blackish
goose with a white spot on its neck. My guide told me quickly
that it was a Brent. My pleasure at this sight, however, was
entirely spoilt when I discovered that the bird had been
wounded for when I got out of my car to investigate further,
the movement I made, quite naturally put most of the ducks
present on the wing but the Brent could not take off as his wing
was damaged.

Unfortunately, because so many of these flooded pitfalls are
situated in comparatively populated places, there is a lot of
indiscriminate shooting. Sundays and Saturdays see groups of
long-haired, young men parading the neighbourhoods, armed
with a most varied assortment of artillery. Air guns, .22 rifles,
twelve bores, both ancient and modern, are carried by car,
motor-cycle, bicycle and on foot to these bird frequented places
where slaughter is then committed. It is easy to get a gun in
these days of the affluent society. Shot guns and air guns require

no special licence for their purchase and such dangerous weapons are now available in general stores and bicycle shops. Guns and rifles can be procured on the hire-purchase system of payment. In some ways it is surprising that there are not more youngsters about raiding the land with their firearms. The pity of the whole thing is that in so many cases anything that flies is shot. Birds have no security from these gunmen of the ponds. The police have attempted to take action but like some horrible recurrent disease these human predators appear to have an everlasting supply of newcomers to replenish those who are infrequently apprehended by the law. I use the word gunmen as these men are in no sense sportsmen. Killing appears to be their pleasure and I doubt very much whether they even eat what they shoot. Men of this type have been occasionally caught with birds like eider ducks, redshanks and thrushes on them. They constitute a menace which should be eradicated but it seems impossible, at present, to do so.

The reverse of the coin may appear surprising for pitfalls, situated on well guarded shoots, can produce not only a wide and varied crop of beautiful birds but also an excellent bag of edible ducks.

Pitfall ponds such as those at Seaton Burn, already mentioned, and another at Holywell near Bedlington, are shot, perhaps two or three times a year, for the mallard, teal and wigeon they can supply; all the rest of the year they are left alone so that you get, as at Holywell, really astonishing records of immensely varied birds many of whom rest and nest there. Most pitfalls situated as they are in coal-mining districts can well be described as jewels of water set in a sad, drear frame of unattractive land.

★ 28 ★

PEGSWOOD MOOR

A REFUSE DUMP may well appear to be an unsavoury place in which to do one's bird watching but that a number of species of birds appreciate its precincts there is no doubt. Sometimes, you can see some interesting avian visitors on these disgusting spots. Pegswood Moor is on the outskirts of the colliery village of Pegswood. I suppose, at one time, there was a wood there but it is no more. It is, in fact, a very barren place. There is little of a moor about Pegswood, although not so very long ago there were considerable stretches of rough ground with occasional patches of dusty heather and long yellow grass. All this has been obliterated and less attractive grass pastures now exist. The earth appears to be perpetually grey. The sheep which graze, in the wire-fenced enclosures, have a dirty look. Rows of council houses fringe the Moor and in the distance, overlooking all, are the huge pit heaps, like a dirty chain of lesser mountains. The slag piles of Ashington are proudly claimed by its inhabitants to be some of the largest coal heaps in the whole of Britain.

The refuse dump of the village of Pegswood is situated to the east of the last row of council houses. There is a ninefoot, wire-mesh fence around the dump. This high barrier makes the place, in the distance, look somewhat like a miniature P.O.W. camp. The fence surrounds the refuse so as to keep out the sheep and the occasional cattle which are in the fields around the place. You cannot just go in and dump your dirt there for all refuse, which is destined for Pegswood Moor, must be placed there by the official refuse disposal officers employed by the council. It is a very exclusive place and many birds love it. They are also quite oblivious of its sanctity.

Stray cats, of which there are a considerable number in the

vicinity, give the refuse dump a wide berth as on numerous occasions they have been severely dealt with by the massed flocks of carrion crows, rooks, jackdaws and herring gulls who regard the Lucullian feast, provided by the refuse heap, as exclusively their own.

There is a convenient side road which passes close to the dump and provided the wind is in the right direction, so that the air is not polluted, it is possible to park one's car clear of the road and with a pair of binoculars to study the birds of Pegswood Moor. You have, as it were, an all-enclosed ringside seat and as the actual cover, about the dump, is scanty the birds present stand out like actors on a platform. I have noted the following species on this stage; rooks, carrion crows, jackdaws, gulls, starlings, peewits, dunnocks, chaffinches, robins, blackbirds, in fact, a very representative gathering of our more common birds. Bird behaviour rather than a search for some unusual species is the forte of Pegswood.

One Saturday in February I was driving north, past the Moor, when I observed an oddly coloured bird, a decided stranger in the neighbourhood. Watching her, I decided she was a Royston crow, a bird which to us in Northumberland is mainly a migrant. She was playing in courtship with a jet-black carrion crow. I noticed she was lame, as she limped here and there amongst the sheep. Because she kept at a respectable distance from the road, I could not definitely confirm my diagnosis, as amongst the gathering of rooks, I had, on several occasions, noted oddly-coloured birds with distinctive white and grey markings. One individual, in particular, had bars of white across both wings and, at a distance, appeared strangely like a magpie.

Wishing to confirm the arrival of the Royston on the Moor, I went up on Sunday morning with a pair of binoculars. I soon found my friend of the previous day and was able to verify that she was the same bird by her limp. There was no doubt as to her identity. She was a fine specimen of the Hooded or Royston crow. Accompanied by her black companion of the day before, she came and perched on a gutted oak close to the car.

The birds, after resting for a while on the oak, both flew into the air, where they proceeded to perform a number of aerial gyrations which took them towards the refuse heap. Diving on to this, the carrion crow picked up a morsel and climbed vertically into the air. Dropping the particle from his beak, he dived again as if to intercept it before it reached the ground. At other times he would pick up some scrap from the dump and climb with it to a height of two or three hundred feet, when he would let it go. After it had hit the ground, he would zoom on to the scrap and tear it with his beak. What there was on the refuse heap which required treatment usually adopted by these birds when feeding on mussels and other molluscs on the seashore I never discovered. The habit is probably instinctive. During these aerobatics on the part of the carrion crow the hoodie would occasionally climb and mix in with him.

Suddenly to my surprise, I noticed what appeared to be another hoodie who flew in from the east above the lame bird and who immediately took to performing a series of antics in the air. Climbing vertically, he would stall in the air to fall tumbling in a series of clumsy rolls, much to the apparent admiration of my lame friend. Meanwhile, the carrion crow also kept up his aerial display. This continued for a period of ten minutes or so, when all three birds, as if by mutual agreement, decided that they had had enough exercise. They came to earth and proceeded to search the nearby dump for pickings. During this process the newly-arrived hooded crow went up to the lame hoodie and nudged her with his beak. She did not resent his approach but hopped into the air with spread wings, to be followed by her new suitor. Meanwhile, her first mate, the carrion bird placidly picked away at the grass within a few feet of the pair.

Suddenly, without any obvious reason, the second hoodie climbed into the air, circled the field once, and set his beak for the south. The last I saw of him, he was a speck in the sky above the railway viaduct.

Next morning I returned to see what the matrimonial situation was and discovered the lame female hooded crow and her carrion mate peacefully feeding amongst their friends, the sheep. I never discovered whether the pair nested, although such matings are not unknown and have occurred within the confines of the county. One lot of nestlings of such a union, on examination, were found to be either pure carrion crows or pure hooded crows. There were no half bred birds amongst the offspring.

The biggest thrill I ever experienced on Pegswood Moor was one day in January. It was bitterly cold with a piercing wind from the north-east. Flakes of snow mingled with pellets of hail had already spread a light mantle of white over the pasture land. It was snug-spying, however, from the inside of a warm, saloon car. Most of the birds, who were apparently suffering from the weather, were not putting up much of a show. Suddenly, I noticed a flock of some 20 or 30 sparrows feeding on the grass verge outside the mesh-wire fence, amongst them was a vivid green bird. In its behaviour it was exactly like the sparrows, rising when they did, flying with them in perfect formation and landing and pecking at the soil just like a garden sparrow. For a minute I thought it might be an odd-coloured finch but when I got my glasses on it I saw it was a budgerigar —a lovely bird in fine feather. It appeared to have been completely and successfully adopted by the drab plumaged sparrows.

BOULMER

I DROVE THE car northwards along the A.1 road in the direction of the old market town of Alnwick. Before reaching the arched, stone bondgate, in the centre of the town, I turned right for the coast. From the fishing village of Boulmer through Longhoughton Steads and Howick Cove to Craster is a stretch of coast particularly favoured, at certain times of year, both by sea birds and land birds.

It was a cold, bitter day towards the end of March. A north-easterly wind came off the grey North Sea bringing with it fine pellets of ice. I parked the car on the dunes just north of the harbour where I thought it would be concealed from all human eyes. There was not a soul in sight. The seashore was quite deserted—except for the birds. The weather was such that few people were likely to venture forth to the coast for pleasure.

From the shelter of the car I could see in a shallow bay below the dunes a drake eider performing a series of slow, thorough ablutions. His dowdy duck swam round in wide circles as if she was admiring her decorative mate. On the rocks, exposed by the withdrawn tide, I counted three pairs of shelducks. Their gaudy plumage showed up brilliantly against the dark colour of the whinstone rocks. The shelduck is an attractive and intriguing bird. Both sexes in their plumage are remarkably alike and it is not easy to distinguish them apart. The shelducks which feed by day on this part of the north-east coast are said to fly back across the whole breadth of England to spend the night on the Solway. I have never been able to learn for certain whether or not this is true. I think it would take a lot of proving. Far out on the fringe of the rocks, where the waves lapped the long rank seaweed, I could see, through my glasses, the heads of six grey seals who seemed to be playing a sort of game of "I spy" with one another about the sea's surface.

The wind cut my face when I came out of the shelter of the warm saloon car. The plaintive *wheep* of a redshank rose above the soft moans of the sea and the wind. A dour canopy of grey cloud covered the whole sky.

Well wrapped up in a short jeep coat and a thick, woollen muffler I started to walk along the dunes overlooking the rocky shore below. Almost at once a woodcock sprang from a clump of maran grass within a few feet of where I walked. The bird pitched three hundred yards away in another tussock. Whilst I was watching the woodcock a great flight of several hundred golden plovers wheeled overhead to finally alight like a single entity, on a ploughed field which came to within a hundred yards or so of the seashore. On examing the plover I found they were the dark northern variety with their black breasts and throats. The birds were almost certainly on migration to the northern tundras where they would break up and nest but that morning they did not appear to be in any hurry to depart—maybe it was too cold further north for it was certainly bitter enough here. I followed a sheep path along the dunes in the direction the woodcock had taken. Six snowbuntings sprang from the grass, they did not go far but settled soon again to explore the earth for some small sustenance. The little birds looked like a lot of butterflys when they were on the wing. They were surprisingly rather difficult to spot amongst the long yellow grass in spite of their decorative black, brown and prominent white plumage.

I nearly stepped on the woodcock before she sprang again. This time the bird did not seem to intend to dawdle for in quick zig-zag flight she made out to sea. I wondered whether the cock was bound for some pine forest in Norway where she would nest—of course I did not know the sex of the bird because it is almost impossible to sex 'cock and especially on the wing.

From where I now stood on the brink of the dunes, near Longhoughton Steads, I could see the lovely little cove of Howick with its perfect sand on which, on this cold day, there was not a single human footmark. The wooded ghyll at the mouth of the Howick burn comes right down to the beach and at high-tide the sea very nearly laps the roots of the trees and bushes. Howick Cove is a very attractive place, later on in the year, for both flycatchers and warblers. It acts as a sort of syphon to the visiting migrants bringing them in from the coast, as it were, eventually to spew them out all over the countryside for procreation purposes.

On that morning in late March the ghyll was full of black-birds and they all seemed to be cocks. I have never seen so many blackbirds about as I have observed this year (1964). They all seem to be on migration and most of them appear to be males. This sort of observation happens now and again when one normally watches birds all the year around. You get years when particular species seem to be very numerous in certain localities. This year it has certainly been a blackbird spring.

A few laggard fieldfares were still clacking about in the fields on the fringes of the wooded dene.

Crossing the virgin beach I made for Cullernose Point. Here there was a nice gathering of waders, oyster-catchers, turn-stones and sanderlings were all still flocked. Around the point itself four fulmars were evidently exploring for possible nesting sites. I never cease to admire the wonderful planing flight of these lovely, grey tubenosed birds. I suppose the fulmar is about the most marvellous natural glider in the world.

Just short of the fishing village of Craster, famed for its kippers and its squire, author and considerable natural his-torian Sir John Craster of Craster, I turned for home. Taking a course parallel with the sea, but slightly inland, I put up a pair of partridges. I have noticed of recent years that partridge are beginning to haunt the coastal dunes in increasing numbers. I wonder if they are taking to the sand and maran grass because it is still free from contamination from chemicals? There were numerous other birds, of course, which I noticed that day such as the various gulls, skylarks and rock pipits. Altogether it was a very satisfactory foray with a most gratifying bag or perhaps I should say tally—count sounds so terribly statistical.

This length of seashore is certainly attractive to a large number of birds. The exposed strip of rocks at low-tide offers a rich feeding ground for the aquatics whilst the cultivated land comes right down to the sand dunes and in the middle of the stretch there is the dene of Howick affording ideal shelter for the lesser birds.

When I got back to my car I was astonished to see another parked close alongside it. There was no one in the vehicle. Its owner certainly had nearly the whole coastline within sight on which to rest his motor-car and yet he, or she chose to pitch it right next to mine. This herd instinct in humans seems to be particularly strong amongst a lot of motorists. Park a car off the road or on the shore and in a short time a flock of others come huddling around. It happened that this day, at the end of March, was a particularly cold, bitter one otherwise I suppose the place might have been like a public car park!

★ 30 ★

FENHAM FLATS

Two HALF-CROWN pieces laid side by side on a half-inch map of Northumberland, with the village of Fenham Mill as the centre of the two discs, would cover, within their two perimeters, some of the finest natural wild-fowl feeding grounds in Britain. This extensive tidal reach consists of a number of named areas, Goswick Sand Rig to the north, The Swad and The Slakes in the middle, with Fenham Flats and The Blacks, to the south. To the townsman this is a desolate spot. The last time I visited Fenham Flats I had with me two visitors from the south, a sense of bleakness seemed to enter their souls for to them there was little attraction about this endless stretch of grey, rain-swept, mud. Looking into the rain, driven by a biting north-easterly wind, the flats appeared to undulate like the sea. One of my companions, a practical man to whom waste land was ever something to put to practical use, exclaimed:

"But this could surely easily be dyked to produce good agricultural land?"

And so I suppose it could. Parts of Holland, North Germany, and even hundreds of years ago our own Suffolk and Norfolk coast-lands, were in no better condition. All these areas have, by the building of sea-brakes and artificial draining ditches, been converted into tolerable pasture.

To the wildfowler, however, and the naturalist such a suggestion savours of desecration rather than reclamation!

The most travelled road, to the fringe of these mudlands, is by Beal where the track commences, across this tidal stretch, to Holy Island and Lindisfarne. At low tide, it is possible to

walk, dryshod, across the Swad by the Pilgrim's Way, to the Island. Before the present causeway was built a cart, or a high axled car, could also make the journey. The new motor causeway through the worst portions of The Swad has now enabled anyone with a car to make the trip at suitable tides.

Fenham Flats have been the haunt of many a famous wild fowler and naturalist. Men like Prideaux Selby, C. M. Adamson, George Bolam, Sir Ralph Payne-Gallwey, Abel Chapman, Geoffrey Watson, and Richard Perry are amongst them. The majority of these men were naturalist fowlers, they shot for sport but they were, at the same time, intensely interested in all that concerned the birds of the flats.

Adamson was one of the first naturalists to understand the plumage mutations of the waders. Chapman, and his lesser known brother Alfred, continued Adamson's investigations into the aspects of seasonal colour variations of these species.

It is interesting to learn, from Adamson's own writings, of the onerous nature of the journey to Fenham from Newcastle upon Tyne in the days gone by. This meant the top of a coach to Belford in mid-winter and then by lane and track to Cornet's Inn which is situated at the end of the Fenham Mill Road.

Cornet's Inn is a hostel no longer. The red tiled roof of the little cottage is weather-worn, creepers encase the walls.

At new moons, and at full moons, Adamson used to go out on to the flats, when the tides were right, to prepare hides, known locally as "fox-holes", in the mud. These pits were then lined with oat straw, the shooter would conceal himself to await the flight of the wigeon, towards the succulent feeding on The Swad, from the sea where the birds had been spending the day.

The procedure of wildfowling has changed little since Adamson's day. The shooter still lies out in his "fox-hole" to await in the dusk or dawn the coming of the fowl.

Punt-gunning was introduced to Holy Island from Norfolk, in 1829, over a century ago. There are still a few punts in operation in the locality.

During the hungry nineteen forties, in the immediate postwar era, when flesh was scarce and most meats were severely rationed, the professional wildfowler, with his mass slaughtering punt-gun, did well. There was a steady demand for all sorts of ducks and waders in the markets of the industrial North.

Space does not permit an attempt to describe the considerable bird life which exists around Holy Island and Fenham Flats. Fortunately, for those who are interested, Richard Perry, an exceedingly painstaking and accurate observer, spent many months on Holy Island studying its birds. The result is that admirable book *A Naturalist on Lindisfarne*. In his book Perry describes the individual birds in detail, his vivid pen paintings of the huge members of some of the species helps one to realise what Fenham Flats are like during the winter months and at the times of bird migration.

Perry has compiled as an Appendix to his book, a systematic list of the birds of Holy Island, this consists of no less than twenty-four pages. The list comprises 256 species and sub-species recorded on Holy Island, the Slakes and Goswick Sands. It is a valuable contribution to the ornithological data on British birds. Few Northumbrians now know of the existence of this work.

The great variety of birds of the Flats is one of the things which strikes a layman most forcibly, from the great whooper swan to the minute gold crest, the smallest of all our birds, they all seem to turn up at one time or another in this vicinity.

Holy Island and its adjacent territories are the age-old resting places for the migratory birds which travel in the spring to their nesting haunts in the far north. In the autumn, their family affairs completed, these vast hordes journey southwards to spend the winter in a warmer climate.

Many of the ducks and geese winter in the neighbourhood. It is this multitude which provides the wildfowler with his sport. The swans, the geese, the ducks, both sea and land, the various waders, they are here in their hundreds and thousands. Fortunately, through a measure of sensible protection and the arrangement of proper close seasons, there would appear, at present, to be little likelihood of a diminution in their numbers.

It is sometimes stated that we, in this country, lag behind other nations in the conservation of our wild life, but there is no country in the world who has, today, amongst its human population a greater number of bird lovers and good sportsmen both of whom are equally anxious to protect this heritage.

★ 31 ★

ABANDONED
RAILROADS

AMONGST THE more rewarding fields for the keen ornithologist are the many miles of abandoned railways which now traverse this country. These derelict swathes of land are often full of birds and other wild life. Derelict is, perhaps, not the right word for now that these lines have reverted to nature they can be very prolific terrain. I have spent many happy hours along the abandoned railroad which used to run from east to west, across the country, less than a mile from where I live. I do not think I have ever visited this strip of land without seeing something to interest me.

When the powers-that-be decide to put a railroad out of action, because it no longer pays, the first thing that usually happens is a removal of the human employees from the many stations, halts and crossings, along the line. This transfer is, in fact, the elimination of an appreciable disturbance element to all wild life. Some of the older employees, and possibly pensionable persons, may decide to stay on, on railway property. Other houses along the line, are let, or otherwise disposed of. When a railway is axed the human element, in and about it, is nearly always appreciably reduced.

The first physical act, once it is decided to stop the trains running, is to remove the steel rails. These presumably go back into the steel melting furnaces for they contain valuable metal. Once rid of the rails the wooden sleepers are dealt with. These are nearly always of selected wood, heavily impregnated with tar. They make good small bridges, gate posts and also, when cut up, fine burning timber. Stripped of its wood and metal the old railroad quickly becomes overgrown. The fences which are all extremely strong and durable, in quality, remain *in situ*, presumably because the property within their limits still belongs to B.R.

When the railroads were originally constructed throughout Britain they were massively built, well-drained and strongly fenced with concrete posts, steel wire and creosoted timber. The fact that most railroad fences still stand intact is a tribute to their sound construction.

An old railway map of the British Isles will show that this country's railroads once ran here and there and almost everywhere throughout the land. They traversed an infinite variety of terrain. As far as possible a rail track had to run straight and as level as possible. This meant that the lines had to be driven through hill and dale, over rivers and even under mountains. Ravines, cuttings, tunnels and embankments were all to be met with along their routes.

The solid fencing, besides these ways, has kept out cattle, sheep and other domestic stock. The inherent fear, in human beings, of encroaching on these places, where once high-speed, smoke-belching engines ran, still exists and even now not many people "trespass" on these derelict lines.

Wild animals and birds find these places excellent habitations. There are no cattle to tramp on ground nests, no mechanical sillage cutters to rip out the cover before the chicks are fledged. No fungicides, herbicides, pesticides, or other noxious and dangerous chemicals are poured on to these useless swathes of land and above all there is usually abundant undergrowth available in which both animals and birds are able to effectively conceal themselves.

Birds like wild patridges and pheasants like these old railroads to nest on and amongst the reasons for their choice is the fact that there are usually excellent dusting conditions available, as well as an abundance of weed seeds and insect life, all free from potent, destructive chemicals. The lesser birds also appear to find the ragged hedgerows which grow along some of these routes desirable nesting quarters. In many other parts of the country modern farming methods have stripped the land of its hedgerows. Thousands of miles of hedges have been scrubbed out during the past ten years. In the process of the destruction of these hedges the nesting sites of both game birds, like the pheasant and the partridge, as well as the passerines have been eliminated. There has, in fact, during the past quarter of a century, been a sort of large scale eviction of hundreds of thousands of our birds. Numbers of these refugees have found our abandoned railroads admirable new quarters.

When I take a walk along my own particular stretch of abandoned track, always with my binoculars, I make a point of walking against the wind so my scent does not flow towards the wild beasts whose noses are so much a part of their defensive mechanism and the sound of one's footsteps is not so easily heard by the birds, some of whom seem to have remarkably acute hearing, as well of course, as sight.

Within the distance of a mile this track runs through fields with wild, unclipped, wind-blown hawthorn trees beside the wire fence alongside the way. A little further on comes a conifer plantation, twice burnt by flying cinders when trains once ran here. It has grown up now and the vivid green larches in spring are particularly favoured by gold crests and blue-tits. After the fir trees there is the old oak wood and why this has never been subjected to fire when the conifers have I have never really understood. Past the oaks open land appears once more until the track wanders, in gradual curves, into the northern, market town which is our shopping centre.

I went up-wind from the empty station yard, through the fields, towards the oak wood. From my elevation on the railroad I could see two cock pheasants, splendid in their shining bronze plumage, battling for territory in the field below. A green woodpecker came towards me undulating along the course of the abandoned railroad yaffling his song. As he dipped and climbed in his see-saw flight he showed off his scarlet cardinal's cap and his olive-green feathers. The ragged hedgerow, below the embankment, held two portly bullfinches their rose-red breasts brilliant in the clear, spring sunlight. A little further on two great tits flirted in and out of the fresh green conifers. The tits were particularly numerous in the area and a party of some fifteen long-tailed tits surprised me for by now most of the birds had paired and were well on with their domestic affairs. A cock yellowhammer, perched on the wire fence, looked as golden as a caged canary.

In the pasture, adjoining the oak wood, two brown hares bounced and circled one another in their pre-mating play.

Advancing along the track the flash of a little, red body in one of the oak trees made me freeze into immobility. The tiny face peered down at me from the fork of the gnarled tree. At first, I thought it was a red squirrel but I quickly realised that I was staring into the jet-black, beady eyes of a stoat. We both stood at gaze until the tiny tree creeper, the stoat had been hunting, flew off on to the bole of another massive oak.

This particular stretch of abandoned railroad is particularly favoured by whinchats, redstarts and wheatears and every year these birds come to nest somewhere along its way. On more than one occasion I have seen all three species quite close together with each pair busily occupied in their own mating affairs.

In a number of places on the rail embankment there was evidence of birds and animals in the form of their droppings, spoor and pellets. Prominently placed on a fresh mole-heap was the white bleached skull of a badger probably placed there by some fox cub for the vulpine tribe had left many of their cards along the track.

Coming down from the railroad to the little hunt-wicket gate which led into the fields I put up a pair of partridges who sprang from the long, yellow grass which grew in luxuriant abundance on the embankment. The old disused railroad, now shorn of its steel rails and wooden sleepers, was a place vibrant with wild-life.

★ 32 ★

BIRDS AND AIRPORTS

THE BIG AIRCRAFT of Flight No. 491 sat on the apron of the airport at Frankfurt awaiting its turn to take off for London. It was already a quarter of an hour behind schedule owing to a heavy congestion of aircraft coming in and taking off. The sun shone in a clear, blue sky. Visibility was exceptionally good.

I had been fortunate enough to get a seat by a window in the stern of the plane. From my seat I had a good view of the surrounding airfield. After another five minutes waiting the aircraft took her place in the queue at the far end of the aerodrome. As we rose over the perimeter of the field I looked out of my window at the ground slipping past us. In a small clearing, in a fir plantation, by the perimeter runway, suddenly, I saw the yellow form of some animal. For a second I thought the creature might be a roedeer. There are plenty of roedeer in the woods around Frankfurt and in the nearby Taurus Mountains. The yellow beast turned out to be a big, light-coloured fox. He was paused, about to pounce on a tuft of grass. The fox was mouseing. The clarity of the whole scene struck me forcibly. The plane I was in was travelling at hundreds of miles an hour; we were climbing fast and yet I could see all this. I wondered if the perspex window beside me had some power of magnification. A few moments later we passed over a glade amongst some tall, black fir trees, a kestrel hovered beneath us. The huge aircraft did not appear to disturb the bird at all. I could see the mottled, rust-red plumage of the bird's back feathers as if it were hovering in a big glass case.

As we were to fly to England at over 20,000 feet it was not long before we left the earth as a distant blur beneath us.

Coming through low cloud to land at Heathrow I could see very little until the plane had almost touched down. As the wheels screeched at their impact with the harsh tarmac two lapwings rose, in tumbling flight, busily occupied in their pre-nuptial love play.

A few days after my Frankfurt-London trip I had to go over to Brussels and Amsterdam. Melsbroek Airport, near Brussels, always appears to me to have a great number of larks on it. This rather surprised me as you do not see a great many of these birds elsewhere in the Belgian countryside. So as to avoid coming home, in between trips, I took a Scandinavian Air Services aircraft from Melsbroek to Schipol. Black-headed gulls were much in evidence around the perimeter of the field. Close to the asphalt runway, on which we landed, were a pair of oyster-catchers. These two handsome black-and-white waders, with their brilliant, orange-coloured beaks and legs, were still in the same place when we took off on a B.E.A. plane two days later. I believe they were nesting amongst the roughness between the runway and the adjoining grassland.

Certain airports are, in my mind, associated with certain birds. When I think of Marseilles I think of its seagulls. Heathrow has its larks, lapwings and in the winter frequent flocks of woodpigeons. Wolsington Airport, near Newcastle upon Tyne, has a number of covies of partridges around its margins. Flying over the North Sea from Dusseldorf to Wolsington one day the pilot came back into the cabin to speak to his passengers. He too had noticed the partridges. He was thinking of having a shot at them over the week-end. I wonder if he ever did. I never saw him again to ask him.

Palma Airport, in Majorca, holds memories for me of a hoopoe and on one occasion a black kite which was obviously hunting the neighbouring almond groves for little birds. It seems that in countries, where trigger-happy sportsmen still shoot little birds all the year round, you often find birds near an airport when they are scarce elsewhere. I have in mind particularly countries like Italy and Spain. The truth is, I think, that human killers are kept off these airfields by the police and airport authorities so that the birds are left in comparative peace.

During the second World War I served in the R.A.F. I spent a lot of time on aerodromes, nearly as much as I spent, chairborne, in an office in London. On some R.A.F. stations birds became quite a problem. Partridges and seagulls in particular would get sucked into the carburettor air-intakes of the Halifax and Lancaster bombers. We had, in certain instances, to design broad-gauge, wire-mesh guards to keep the remains of birds out of the interior of the engines. Engine failure, during take-off, might well result in a "write-off". I think I am right in saying that all the Lancasters, used on the low-level bombing raids on the German dams, were equipped with these air-intake guards to prevent the possibility of birds, suddenly rising from the ground, coming into collision with these low-flying aircraft. These precautions were taken, not necessarily for protection in and around the precincts of airfields, but mainly because these particular aircraft had a special job of low-level flying to do.

During the second World War the problem of preventing collision with birds on aerodromes became quite a major one. A senior officer of the R.A.F. was appointed to explore the possibilities of keeping airfields free of avian life. The problem was far from an easy one to solve. Shooting on the aerodromes was encouraged. Attempts were made to try to fly trained hawks at birds in the vicinity of the R.A.F. stations.

There are, of course, a number of reasons why both birds and wild animals are to be found on, and in the neighbourhood of, airfields. Hares are often to be seen on aerodromes for they know that these places are almost like sanctuaries. Dogs are not encouraged, and man the arch-predator, unless he has a specific job to do on a busy airfield, is not permitted either. It is the comparative peace from interference which makes these places popular with wild life.

One day when I was waiting for a long delayed plane to arrive at Wolsington Airport. I took a stroll around the

perimeter of the field. I had not gone very far before two Airport policemen picked me up. Unauthorised people were not
permitted to wander about the place and quite right too.

Birds and beasts both quickly get used to the noise and the
disturbance of the atmosphere by huge, flying aircraft. Providing the landing and take-off strips are avoided there is much
land about which is undisturbed. It is on this land that birds
and animals can live in peace. Around most aerodromes there
is a considerable area of ground where humans are not allowed,
these margins around the flying ground often afford good cover
for wild life, as well as admirable nesting places for such birds
as curlews, lapwings, larks and partridges.

The fox I saw on the perimeter of Frankfurt Airport obviously knew where he was likely to be safe to pursue his own
hunting of mice undisturbed.

Birds, unless they are particularly large specimens, hardly
constitute much of an air risk nowadays. Modern planes are
so big, massive and powerful that in the event of a collision a
little puff of dust and a few feathers is all that is likely to remain
for a second in the air—but wild birds and beasts are scarcely
fools, most of them know enough to keep clear of the tarmac.

★ 33 ★

THE MENACE OF OIL

A KINGFISHER, with its plumage severely oiled, was recently brought to the London Zoo for treatment by a well-intentioned person who had discovered the bird in this condition. Kingfishers are one of our most lovely birds. I never cease to wonder at the glorious sheen of the various blues and red browns which go to make up the colour pattern of the kingfisher's plumage. An oiled kingfisher must be a particularly pathetic sight. At the same time any bird which has been subjected to an immersion in oil is something greatly to be pitied. Oiled birds appear to be so utterly helpless. Their attempts to preen off the oil on their feathers with their beaks is such a futile proceeding which rarely, if ever, is successful.

I live on a part of the coast where oil is a perpetual menace to the birds of our seas. I have seen oiled birds of many marine species. I have, however, not come across many cases of birds who have suffered from oil pollution in fresh waters. The kingfisher, however, was not, by any means, a rare victim of the oil menace. Swans on the river Thames are frequent sufferers. The upset of an oil barge recently in the Thames caused a number of casualties. The swans soused in oil were treated with sawdust to absorb the viscous fluid. They were then bathed with soap solvents and kept in confinement for a period of recuperation. In spite of this careful treatment it was not possible to entirely cleanse the birds of their covering of black oil.

Amongst the birds, I have found on the seashore, who have

succumbed as a result of the presence of oil, are the various gulls, herring, blackheaded, black-backed and common. Guillemots and puffins are frequent casualties, mainly because of their habit of swimming and diving rather than doing much flying. A police sergeant rang me up one evening to tell me he had picked up a most unusual dead bird on Cresswell beach. From his description, over the 'phone, I thought it might be a little auk. It proved, when I saw it, eventually, to be a young puffin which had been so severely contaminated with oil that it was almost unrecognisable. Little auks often perish as a result of having been in contact with oil. One of the less common fatalities, I found on the beach, possibly because they are not very numerous, was a young red-throated diver who had perished from an overdose of oil on its immature plumage.

Gannets appear to be particularly prone to oiling. I do not think these birds wittingly dive into oil, where it is present on the surface of the water, but they may, after completing their dive, surface in patches of oil.

Both the scoter and the eider ducks often suffer from oil. In their case, too, as diving ducks, who spend a great deal of their time at sea, they are continually running the risk of oil contamination.

The prolonged period of suffering which sea-birds undergo before they eventually succumb to the oil menace was, recently, forcefully brought to my notice when I was on the sea-shore a few miles north of the mouth of the river Blyth. The ports of Newcastle, Tynemouth, the two Shields and Blyth have a regular traffic through them of oil-burning vessels; these constitute a constant threat to the bird life of the adjacent coast-lines. As I stood on the beach watching the breakers on a receding tide I saw an object which, at first, I took to be a floating black bottle. An examination, through my binoculars, disclosed a severely oiled sea-bird which I was able to distinguish as a guillemot. The bedraggled bird was vainly trying to struggle against the powerful surge of the receding sea. Weakened, by the black oil on its wings and the down on its belly, the bird was finally caught by the tidal breakers. As each wave broke over the guillemot the bird was tossed here and there in the surf until it could hardly keep its swimming poise. After clearing a wave, it would sit on its tail, in the water, vainly trying to preen the wing feathers of their coating of filthy, clinging, black oil. The bird's pathetic flapping became weaker as the sea drove the derelict shorewards. A wave, more boisterous than usual, turned the sea-bird over and over and, in its retreating, left the guillemot stranded. Gaining its feet, the bird struggled weakly up the wet beach. Making towards the guillemot I heard, overhead, the raucous voice of a carrion crow. A pair of these birds, hunting the foreshore, had spotted the guillemot in its distress. I found the guillemot was in a bad way. There was little chance of its survival. I put the bird out of its misery, as quickly as I could, with a blow from my walking-stick aimed at the base of the skull. Left to the crows its end could scarcely be thought of. My presence on this occasion was perhaps fortuitous as I was able to put this pitiful bird out of its misery, for the truth is that most birds which have become subject to the evil of floating oil suffer a prolonged death through starvation and its attendant weakness. Some of them, however, become the victims of the carrion feeders such as the carrion crows when their misery is prolonged before being finally, horribly terminated.

★ 34 ★

BIRD CASUALTIES OF OUR ROADS

IT HAD RAINED without stopping for three whole days and nights. The countryside was drenched. Moisture dripped from the trees. The hedgerows were damp places. Sodden carpets of green grass covered the fields.

Then the sun came out from behind the low, grey ceiling of clouds, bringing with it the warmth of a summer day. The road was the first place in the land to dry. Within an hour of the sunlight coming there were dry patches on the hard surface of asphalted granite chips. Here and there pools of water remained where the road had sunk. Most of the highway dried quickly as the ditches along the roadside had been well maintained.

The road was cared for by the R.D.C. roadman, who spent his days attending to its wants. The roadman was a skilled ditcher, he knew the value of efficient drainage. Occasionally, however, a ditch would clog when an unmanageable mass of twigs, leaves, and other detritus of the roadside, formed miniature dams in the roadway. Then the road became flooded and the fast moving traffic would send up from its rubber-shod wheels great sprays of water.

Like a long magnet of blue-grey steel the road attracted to itself the wild-life of the countryside. After three days of wet the birds came forth from their damp perches in the trees and hedges and from out of the fields to dry their bedraggled plumage on the highway. Within a distance of a mile eight different kinds of birds had congregated. A pair of partridges, with their nest washed out, had come through the grass verge to sun themselves. Two carrion crows pecked voraciously at the squashed carcase of a hedgehog. Four yellowhammers kept up a frolicking flight above the swiftly drying metalled way. A cock blackbird bridled at his hen, relieved that the deluge had ceased. Two wagtails ducked and ran around the quickly receding water in the road pools. A family of thrushes, the youngsters fresh from their nest, were crouching beneath the grass edge as if they were trying to suck the warmth of the road into their bodies.

With the increasing heat of the sun the insects hatched out. Swallows coursed the lanes, seeking easy sustenance from the myriads of flying things hardly visible to the human eye. The swallows were ravenous after three days of steady downpour. Here and there a swallow would cease from its hunting to squat with its breast pressed down on to the rough warm surface of the highway.

The rain had washed the hedges of their coating of dust and green leaves were vivid in their cleanliness. The rapidly evaporating clouds left behind them a clear, depthless blue sky. The smells of the cleansed earth rose in swathes from the warm corridors of the road. The radiant heat from the asphalt surface attracted still more beasts and birds, all of whom appeared to be oblivious of the perils of the high-speed traffic lane.

The toll of death on the road was heavy that morning. Even some of the predators, like the carrion crows and the magpies, usually crafty creatures, nearly succumbed to the swiftly moving vehicles, for they had already gorged on the earlier casualties of the road. The carrion birds, being exceedingly wily creatures, were normally rare victims of the traffic, it rather was the young and inexperienced members of the wild who made up the greater part of the road's toll.

The mortality of birds on our modern roads amounts to a huge figure every year. It is, of course, practically impossible to assess the actual number of casualties with any degree of accuracy. The peak periods of accident, however, would appear to take place during courtship prior to nidification. The highways can then be exceedingly dangerous for birds who are mostly absorbed in their mating conquests and display.

The highways of Britain are attractive places for birds because a great many roads have fine bordering hedges which provide excellent nesting sites; moreover, fast modern motor traffic kills, as well as birds, other forms of life such as insects and mammals. Insects are welcome food to many species of birds, dead animals provide good feasting to the crows, gulls and other carrion feeders. After a period of rain roads are quickly drained. The sun dries them before the surrounding countryside. Birds come to the roads to dry themselves and feel their warmth.

Nearly every day of the week I motor 15 miles to my work along secondary roads where the traffic density is by no means great; in spite of this fact it is surprising the number of dead and wounded birds I come across. During the present week I have recovered three different species, a song thrush, a rook, and a hen blackbird. The song thrush was dead but the others were severely injured so that I had to put them out of their misery as quickly as possible. If the bird mortality of the roads I travel nearly every day, is typical then the death rate on *all* the roads of Britain must reach huge figures.

Many of the less badly damaged dead birds, I have picked up, eventually serve a useful purpose. This is because one day, after I had found a particularly fine specimen of a cock yellow-hammer, I took it into the Hancock Natural History Museum in Newcastle upon Tyne as I thought the bird might possibly be of some use to them. I am glad I did so as the Curator was delighted with my specimen.

"We are most anxious to get as many of these little birds, in good, fresh condition, as we can", he said. "We set them up and lend them to schools for educational purposes."

Because the majority of our smaller, wild birds are now properly protected by the 1954 Bird Protection Act and its amendments such specimens are not easy to obtain.

I realised, at once, that the mortality of the roadways I traversed might well supply a useful purpose. The variety of birds already handed into the Museum include a rook, a jack-

daw, a dunnock, a linnet, a sand martin, song-thrushes, blackbirds, chaffinches and yellowhammers.

Over a period of time it has been possible to make a survey
of the cause of death of many of these road victims. A surprising
large percentage of birds appear to die from head-on collisions.
Skull damage predominates with wing injury coming next. I
have no doubt that many birds with broken or dislocated wings
limp off the roads into the road verges and hedgerows where
eventually they fall victims to rats, cats, stoats and weasels.
Quick death by collision would seem to be preferable to the
eventual lot of these maimed birds.

The motorist himself is seldom to blame for killing a bird on
the road for at times, and particularly during the mating period,
birds fly straight into cars and lorries. Chaffinches, yellowhammers and blackbirds appear to be amongst the most careless "jay-flyers". Incidentally I wonder why humans who are
careless of traffic are called "jay-walkers". The jay is a very
crafty bird. He certainly is no frequenter of the dangerous
roads!

Some of these deaths on the road have a remarkable poig-
nancy about them. I noticed a dead hen yellowhammer, one
morning, by the roadside, beside her stood the cock bird, he just
did not seem to realise what had happened to his mate. On
another occasion I picked up a freshly killed linnet, for a
moment, I thought the rosy flush on his neck was dried blood,
in the bird's beak was firmly grasped a small tuft of red heifer's
hair which he was carrying to line the nest with.

A case of apparent bravery happened within a mile from my
house. I came around a wide bend in the road to see in front of
me a weasel dragging the corpse of a cock yellowhammer across
the asphalt. Diving at the weasel, in active rushes, was the hen
bird as if she were striving to regain possession of the dead body
of her mate.

It is, I think, nearly always best to destroy quickly a badly
damaged bird if you can bring yourself to do so. But sometimes
such a course is hard to follow.

I remember once coming across a golden plover with a
broken wing. It was being chased along the side of the road by a
dog. I stopped the dog and managed to recover the bird.

Seldom have I handled a more beautiful creature. I took it into
the car meaning to put it out of its misery. Once in the car the
bird settled on the seat beside me apparently quite unafraid.
I could not bring myself to kill that plover. I took it to a nearby
pond and released it amongst the rushes. Perhaps it was a silly,
sentimental thing to do as undoubtedly, in its injured state, it
would eventually succumb to the beak, teeth, or claws, of some
predator.

★ 35 ★

SOME BIRDS
OF MALLORCA

THE BALEARIC ISLANDS are now a short journey by air from London. It takes a little over three hours to reach Son San Juan airport, in the island of Mallorca, from Heath Row.

Mallorca has a small resident population of Britishers many of whom have chosen this island for its climate and economical living. Additionally Mallorca has an ever increasing influx of British tourists. Many of these visitors come in the summer and spring but this traffic is also on the increase in the early months of the year.

There appears to be a general impression amongst both tourists and residents that the Mallorcans are a trigger-happy community anxious to shoot anything that flies. This is largely a fallacy. Cartridges are expensive in Mallorca, as they are here, and the natives certainly do not let off their guns at all and sundry. I have met a number of Mallorcan sportsmen and their main quarries seem to be partridges, hares, duck, most of the waders, blackbirds, thrushes and larks. It is the last-named, poor man's game, which has, I feel, contributed largely to the trigger-happy credo.

Mallorcans shoot a lot of thrushes, and particularly during the months of January and February, when the island appears to be visited by flocks of these birds. We shoot migrant woodcock here in Britain when they arrive in November and December from over the North Sea. The Balearic Islanders kill thrushes and consider them as succulent morsels as some of us consider woodcocks. Thrushes are hung up for sale in many greengrocers and comestible shops, just as game is displayed for sale in our poulterers' shops.

Another bird which is severely dealt with by the islanders is the hawfinch and this can be readily understood when one has seen an orange grove with its ripe fruit attacked after a visit from these birds.

The so-called curved-beaked, clawed birds are seldom shot. Kites, eagles, ospreys and kestrels are to be seen in many parts of Mallorca and they appear to be quite unmolested. I am not suggesting that a shepherd will not destroy an eagle or its nest should he find his flock suffering.

Stuffed birds in glass cases, as a form of household decor, are as unfashionable in Mallorca as they are in this country, so that there is no need to kill birds to stuff them. Wild birds are still trapped for cage purposes and there are shops in Palma who do a thriving business in these pathetic captives but then it was not so very long ago that the same thing was happening in Britain.

I was glad I had decided to take a pair of binoculars with me when I visited Mallorca this year for without them I would have missed the enjoyment of observing a number of birds which were comparatively unknown to me until then.

The first place I stayed at was C'as Catala a short bus-ride from Palma. Taking a stroll along the shore that evening I was delighted to get a view of a hoopoe, a Kentish plover and a flight of some thirty Balearic shearwaters.

The hoopoe is a common bird in the island and it is certainly —next to the house sparrow—one of the tamest. The hoopoe to me is always a thrilling bird to see with its brilliant plumage and its curious undulating flight not unlike that of the British woodpeckers.

I had never seen a Kentish plover before as in England the range of this bird is confined to a small part of the south-east coastal mainland. This tiny plover, for it is not much larger than the common house sparrow, has an extensive breeding range around the coasts of Europe and the Mediterranean.

The Balearic shearwater has now received sub-specific status although until comparatively recently the shearwaters of the Balearic Isles were regarded as identical to our Manx shearwaters. The Balearic bird has been named *Procellaria puffinus mauretanicus*. Shearwaters are numerous around the coasts of Mallorca and the lesser island of Ivitza. Their breeding haunts

are usually in the tiny rocky islets which adorn the coasts of
the Balearic Isles. The sight of three such unusual birds, in
one evening, was certainly a good start for anyone interested in
birds.

The next morning, in brilliant sunlight, I took a stroll up
into the foothills behind my hotel. The land at C'as Catala rises
steeply from the rocky foreshore and the vegetation on the hills
is a composite of many mixed shrubs and conifers. Considering
the sparseness of the soil the density of the vegetation, in places,
is quite remarkable.

I was speedily rewarded by the sight of a pair of tiny Marmora warblers darting here and there in a locust tree. The birds
appeared quite oblivious of my presence whilst they proceeded
with their courtship play. The Marmora is a striking little bird
with its bright orange-coloured legs and scarlet rimmed eyes.
A little later I was able to watch two Sardinian warblers, in a
pine tree. After a brief display of aerial acrobatics the two birds
perched close together side-by-side on a branch to rub bills.
The Sardinian, like the Marmora, is a handsome bird in his
grey and white plumage with dark black cap, there is something
distinctively svelte about the Sardinian's appearance. The
Balearic Islands are particularly rich in their warblers and
during my visit I saw numerous warblers some of which I was
at a loss to identify and particularly such birds as the Cetti's and
Savi's warblers.

Shortly after seeing the Sardinians a mixed flight of serins and
citril finches came past me to settle by a pool of stagnant water
on the path. After a quick sip at the water the birds took wing
again heading westward towards the coast. Some of the serins
were almost as yellow as canaries and, because of their attractive plumage, these little finches are sometimes trapped and
sold as cage birds. However, they are not as highly regarded, by
the natives, as the gold finch which is the most popular of the
Balearic, wild, cage-birds.

The following day I went up again into the hills. At an altitude of approximately 1000 feet I was rewarded by an excellent
view, against the sheer face of a ravine, of a blue rock-thrush.
The male bird of this species is an almost indescribable slate,
blue-grey in colour but the hen, to the layman's eye, is not

easily distinguished from a female blackbird. The blue rock-thrush has an alarm call-note very like that of the blackbird.

A little further up I put up a pair of red-legged partridges. These birds are highly prized by the local sportsmen and a number of them are annually trapped, and are put in small slatted cages eventually to be used as decoys. During this walk, as on my two previous ones, I saw a considerable number of the smaller birds including such attractive species as crossbills and stonechats.

Mallorca is also rich in the raptores and particularly in the mountainous regions between Pollensa and Colobra. A good motor road now connects the seaport of Pollensa and the tiny village of Colobra and this road is shortly to be extended over the hills to the port of Soller on the western shores of the island. Golden eagles have been recorded and both Bonelli's and the booted eagle have been seen. In the cultivated valleys between the mountain ridges kites are far from rare. The Egyptian vulture has been noted in Mallorca and on one occasion I had a glimpse of a bird which I thought might be of this species but was unable definitely to verify my observation. Black vultures are almost numerous.

There are many of the commoner British birds to be seen in the Balearic Islands, the robin, the wren, the chaffinch, the blue-tit, the great tit, the white wagtail and the raven amongst them. Some of these birds, however, and particularly the more brightly coloured ones, such as the blue-tits and great tits, appear to be even more brilliant in their plumage than their counterparts in this country; this may possibly be due to the clarity of the islands' atmosphere and the bright sunlight.

A mention of the birds of the Balearic Islands, without a reference to the late Captain P. W. Munn, would be out of place, for it was Captain Munn who first brought to the notice of the various world-wide ornithological associations the wealth of the bird-life of these islands. Captain Munn spent much of his time, whilst resident in the Balearics, studying birds. Fortunately he has left to posterity, in the form of copious notes, his comments and observations, these may be seen today in the Bird Room at the British Museum (Natural History), Cromwell Road, London, S.W.7.

The amateur ornithologist who visits Mallorca has a wide choice of good places to stay in whilst engaged in bird-watching. Soller in the north-west part of the island is particularly good, ospreys can usually be seen as well as eagles over Puig Maya and many of the lesser birds in the surrounding citrus plantations.

Paguera, C'as Catala, Deya and Valdermosa are all ornithologically interesting. Pollensa has many species of duck on the side waters of its bay. Undoubtedly, however, in my opinion the marshland of Alcudia has all the others beaten for this area is still a primitive place, unfrequented by man and it is, as well, desirable terrain for numerous species of birds both large and small.

★ 36 ★

THE MARSHES OF ALCUDIA

The ancient town of Alcudia, built on the tongue of land which divides the wide, shallow Bay of Pollensa from the sandy beaches of Alcudia, in the island of Mallorca, has been both in turn a Roman and a Moorish city. The place is full of archaeological interest. Behind the beaches of the Bay of Alcudia lie the extensive swamp known as La Albufera. Long since the Romans departed from Alcudia, and within this present century, the British, in the form of an English industrial concern, once undertook to reclaim these vast marshes. In the past this swampland was used as a breeding place for wild bulls for the Spanish bull-rings but today, fortunately for the ornithologist, they are extinct.

Before the work of reclamation was completed the English company went bankrupt. One can appreciate the reason for their insolvency when one sees the preliminary work which was done by this firm, for it is magnificently grandiose in its character. However, it was neither for its archaeological interest nor for an examination of the skilled work of past British engineers that I recently went to Alcudia. I had been told that the bird life of the Alcudia swamp was well worth a visit.

It is easy, today, to reach La Albufera from any of the towns in the island of Mallorca. A good road runs, through a belt of scrub, consisting of Corsican pine, lavender, rosemary, cactus, genista and erica arborea, alongside the Bay of Alcudia within site of the swamp itself. From Pollensa or Alcudia one can hire a car and spend a day, or half a day, in this fascinating place for approximately £1. This is the way I did it. I was so taken by the attraction of La Albufera that I went there more than once when I was staying in Pollensa during the month of February. The place undoubtedly grows on one.

Just after leaving the town of Alcudia the road runs alongside the Lago Grande. In spite of its somewhat grand name the Lago Grande, or Great Lake, is, in fact, a shallow pan of brackish water only a few acres in extent. The most prominent features of the lake are the remarkable numbers of shooting hides which have been erected in and around it. The Lago Grande and its shores appear to bristle with hides. Any wildfowl coming in to alight on its water, during the shooting season, must feel like a lone German raider over London during the later stages of the last war when London was armed to the teeth.

In attempting to drain the swamp area the English had driven long straight canals through the land and with the material excavated from these draining ditches they erected dykes. As a result it is now possible to walk along these dykes into all parts of the swamp. The only habitation within the actual swamp area itself is a papermill. The reeds from the marshes being used for the manufacture of quality, parchment paper.

Trees have grown along certain stretches of these dykes. They are now the favourite haunts of all sorts of flycatchers and warblers. There were so many varieties about, on the occasions I visited Albufera, that I was quite unable to verify them all. I did, however, notice many Sardinian warblers, blackcaps and fantails.

Parts of the swamp and particularly some stretches adjacent to the road itself, have been turned into paddy-fields for the growing of rice.

A small business in salt-recovery also goes on in the marshes

as the water is highly saline but the human element in this
industry appears trivial and its disturbance to the bird-life
seems to be negligible.

The rice paddys and salt pans were empty of human life
when I was in the marshes. Snipe, plover and starlings were
about in considerable numbers and I noted two common sand-
pipers. The birds beside the road were exceedingly wary and
even the approach of a car would put the birds on wing. I was
told by the driver of my hired car that shooting within the limits
of the Albufera marshes was PROHIBIDO but I had not gone
very far on foot into the swamplands themselves when I found
evidence of shooting in the form of frequent empty shot-gun
shells.

Within a few minutes of entering the marshland I saw a
marsh-harrier winging its way towards me at an altitude of a
few feet above the tall rushes. It was an unforgettable sight.
Later that morning I counted no less than twelve marsh-
harriers circling above the marshes of Albufera at the same time.
One wonders how it is possible for there to be so many of the
lesser birds in this area when one realises the numbers of raptores there are and the almost constant shooting that seems to
go on. The truth is, of course, that there is an enormous potential feeding area in these marshes, almost unlimited cover, and
abundant, comparatively safe, nesting places. Many of the
birds I saw about Albufera, however, were doubtless migratory
species who would eventually nest elsewhere.

Before I left the marshes on my first visit I saw herons,
moorhens and mallards. The most pleasant sight of the day
happened on my way back to my hotel for whilst passing the
shallow, sea bay of Pollensa we saw great rafts of ducks floating
on a sea like the proverbial mirror—amongst this congregation
I noted, shoveller, scaup, pochard, and rather surprisingly
numerous coots.

Last winter I went to Alcudia again. This time I had hired
a small 600 c.c. Seat so that I had all the time in the world to
spend in the marshes.

Driving along the coastal road, which passes the Lago
Grande, I found the shallow waters were alive with birds.
Shelduck, mallard, pochard, wigeon and tufted ducks floated

on the lake's surface in closely packed rafts. It was a veritable
encyclopaedia of the anatidae.

On the shooting butts, in the middle of the Lago Grande,
cormorants clustered, in heraldic attitudes, drying their wings
or digesting their meals, whichever reason it is which causes
these ugly black divers to assume these postures. Herring gulls
and black-headed gulls clamoured in the bright, blue sky
above. Several hundred coots and a lone crested grebe, looking
rather like some marine cobra, floated on the dead-calm surface of the brackish shallows.

Looking across the Lago Grande from the window of the car
a marsh harrier appeared suddenly, in wavering flight, above
the tall papyrus reeds on the far side of the lake. Taking my
binoculars to the bird I saw, above the marsh harrier, another
raptore. This was a kite soaring high up in the air searching here
and there for some trifling piece of offal.

It was the sudden noise of the bird striking the water which
drew my attention to the osprey. The osprey was struggling,
with wings extended, to lift itself out of the lake. With much
splashing the bird surfaced to display a large, silver-white fish
clasped in its talons. Climbing in wide spirals into the sky the
osprey set its course for the hills above the tiny village of La
Puebla but the bird never reached its destination for the gulls
now rose, in a cluster, to mob the angler. The osprey strove to
gain altitude and it looked as if the bird was going to get away
with it when six snow-white shapes, flying in perfect, line-astern,
formation, came up from the papyrus reeds on broad, blunt
wings to cut their way through the mobbing gulls straight up
towards the osprey. Seeing the approach of the little egrets the
osprey now dropped his fine, glistening, silver fish into the reed
beds beside the Lago Grande. The egrets having successfully
made the osprey abandon his prize now descended in a
long, sweeping dive in search of the fallen fish. The osprey,
robbed of his catch, continued to climb towards the distant
hills.

Watching this enthralling aerial robbery I was reminded that,
once upon a time, alleged osprey feathers were highly prized
embellishments for ladies' hats, but that, in actual fact, these
so-called osprey plumes were the crest feathers of the egret

family many of whom were slaughtered in their thousands, for the human female's adornment.

Egrets and an osprey—I could not help wondering whether there was something symbolic in this recent affray and that the snow-white, little egrets were out to get their own back on their one-time, fatal pseudonym.

★ 37 ★

SOME BIBLIOGRAPHY ON
ORNITHOLOGY

THE CITY OF Newcastle upon Tyne, like many other provincial English cities, has a most excellent public library. On a recent visit there I took the opportunity of inspecting the shelves where the bird books resided. There were over 300 volumes, mostly of current literature, on the subject of ornithology. How many more there were upstairs in the reference library I do not know but I would guess that there were as many there as downstairs. This mass of print is but a tithe of all the books that have been written on the subject of birds.

Amongst the books in the library I found a most interesting catalogue of bird books which listed 180 volumes shown at an exhibition arranged by the National Book League in 1952. The compiler of this list, one Raymond Irwin, comments that in addition to the books specifically mentioned therein, there were a further 200 volumes which were all still in print at the time of the exhibition. For anyone desiring to make a collection of books on ornithology this is a useful guide.

Most people, when they are interested in a particular subject, like to read as much as they can about it but I doubt whether it would be possible for any one individual person to get through *all* the books which have been written in the English language on ornithology.

Over a period of years the majority of us have accumulated

183

some books concerning the subject which is our main interest. Reading about the things one is keen on often improves one's knowledge of them, gives one new ideas and widens one's horizons.

Books about birds cover a vast field. There are the decidedly technical works which are perhaps more for the specialist. Then there are the books of reference and again there has been, for many years now, the pocket book variety which has been designed to assist the observer in the field. Personal books, of an autobiographical nature, can be very interesting and particularly should they deal with a species, or species, with which one is especially concerned. There are also a lot of local books about the birds of certain districts and practically every county in the British Isles has had some sort of work devoted to its avian residents and visitors.

It is, of course, quite impossible in a brief chapter like this, to mention even all the books of one's own choice. There are bound to be omissions and certainly there will be disagreements as to the value of what has been included and what might well have been left out.

Witherby's *The Handbook of British Birds* by H. F. Witherby, F. C. R. Jourdain, Norman Ticehurst and Bernard W. Tucker, in five volumes, has been referred to as the current work of reference on British birds but there are a number of others of this type. Some of them are perhaps a little out of date but they make admirable reading and I have had much delight in my constant references to The Reverend F. O. Morris' seven volumes entitled *British Birds*. It has been the custom to deride Morris for his acceptance of much second-hand information about various species and one critic has said that Francis Orpen Morris is too didactic to be scientific—this may be, but at the same time the Reverend is a most readable author on any species he chooses to discuss. F. O. Morris' books have gone into several editions. I have two complete sets, one in seven volumes and the other in eight, both, incidentally, picked up very cheaply in second-hand book shops. These books are becoming increasingly valuable, not so much because of their reading matter but because of their many delightful coloured prints of birds.

The Birds of Great Britain by John Gould, published in five volumes, is particularly well illustrated with fine plates and copies of this work are now collectors' pieces.

An early reference series on ornithology, which is still sometimes referred too, is William Yarrell's *A History of British Birds*. Published first in three volumes in 1837 it was considered the principal reference work of the nineteenth century and it went into a number of subsequent editions. In 1901 J. E. Harting who was, at one time, the editor of *The Field* wrote a so-called handbook which he entitled *A Handbook of British Birds*. This is a somewhat bulky book and certainly cannot be carried about in one's pocket.

The most recent reference series on British birds is *The Birds of the British Isles* by David Armitage Bannerman. Illustrated by that delightful bird artist the late George E. Lodge, who unfortunately died before the work was completed, it is a pleasure to dip into. At the time of writing volume twelve is still due to come out.

It was realised by a number of publishers, earlier on in this present century, that there was a need, particularly amongst amateur ornithologists, for a compact sort of pocket-size book on our birds. Something, in fact, which one can take about when travelling by car, air or bicycle. In this field I must say that I have found Collins' publication *A Field Guide to the Birds of Britain and Europe*, written by that trio of eminent ornithologists Peterson, Mountfort and Hollom, to be an invaluable *vade mecum*. When I travel it is part of me. Goodness knows how many editions have been produced and into how many languages this very useful little book has been translated. My own copy has travelled thousands of miles with me but being of stout British construction it is hardly tattered at all in spite of being constantly referred to.

Other little books I am fond of are James Fisher's works published in the Penguin series on *Bird Recognition* which I have had bound as one volume in stout covers. It is now one of my bedside books. Fisher is a most lucid writer and he must have proved a valuable help to a lot of beginners in the world of bird watchers.

Another little book I like is Dr. E. A. R. Ennion's *The British*

Bird, mainly, perhaps, because of its delightful sketches. Ennion today is one of our best bird illustrators, few artists can get the character of a bird with such simple artists' materials and with such economy of line.

Because of their very considerable numbers it is quite impossible to list the books which have been written about individual species, and the birds of a particular area, but most bird lovers at some time or another will wish to own or refer to books of this sort.

In my case, as I live in the far north of England I have naturally gone for our local works. *The Birds of Northumberland and the Eastern Borders* by George Bolam is just the sort of thing a local naturalist needs as is George W. Temperley's *History of the Birds of Durham*. Both books are the work of most competent ornithologists and are very valuable for one who is interested in the birds about the place. *The Birds of Scotland* is another work which covers a limited area but this time a whole country. The joint authors of this book the Misses Baxter and Rintoul are famed for their accuracy and detailed observation of the birds of Scotland. I would say for any keen bird watcher, resident north of the Border, that this book would be a "must".

Collins have published a number of books, in their New Naturalist Monographs, on individual species. *The Yellow Wagtail* by Stuart Smith, *The Redstart* by John Buxton, *The Greenshank* by Desmond Nethersole Thompson, *The Wren* by F. A. Lowe are examples. There is also a quite fascinating book by the same publishers on *Sea-Birds* written jointly by the authors James Fisher and R. M. Lockley.

The sort of book about birds which one can sit down and read continuously is, perhaps, best described as the narrative type. Charles St. John's *The Wild Sports and Natural History of the Highlands*, John Colquhoun of Luss's *The Moor and the Loch* are the sort of thing I have in mind. In this sphere, too, local works are always interesting and often valuable. In Northumberland the late Abel Chapman wrote some attractive books dealing with the birds of the district such as *The Borders and Beyond*, *Bird Life of the Borders*, and *Retrospect*. Probably the most famous book of this sort, that has ever been published, is Gilbert White's *The Natural History of Selborne*. For sentimental reasons alone a copy, I feel, should be included in every bird lover's library.

To a man of limited means it would appear that the possession of a reference work of the type of Witherby and/or Bannerman is valuable. Collins' handbooks, for work in the field, and Fisher's Penguin-Pelicans would help to form a nucleus and then let the collector go his own way for there is so much to choose from. I love browsing through the shelves of secondhand booksellers for the quest for a particular book on birds, or the discovery of some ancient gem of ornithological literature, is almost as exciting, at times, as the sight of a rare and beautiful member of our avifauna.

INDEX